THE
~WORLD~
VEGETARIAN
COOKBOOK

Designed by Philip Clucas MSIAD

....

Photographed by Peter Barry

....

Edited by Jillian Stewart

....

5121 The World Vegetarian Cookbook
Copyright © 1999 Quadrillion Publishing Ltd
Godalming, Surrey, England GU7 1XW

This edition produced for Prospero Books,
a division of Chapters Inc.

ISBN-1-55267-335-9

Printed and bound in Dubai

THE
~ WORLD ~
VEGETARIAN
COOKBOOK

PROSPERO
B·O·O·K·S
A DIVISION OF CHAPTERS INC.

CONTENTS

CONTENTS

Introduction

It's official, vegetarianism is on the increase. Over the last few decades, a revolution in eating habits has taken place that has seen the number of vegetarians in both the United States and Great Britain rise enormously. Contrary to what many people believe, however, the vegetarian diet is not a 20th-century phenomenon. Its current popularity may be a product of today's concern with the damage we are inflicting on our planet and the creatures we share it with, but it is by no means a recent development, and certainly not one limited to the Western hemisphere.

Scientific evidence suggests that our early ancestors existed on a diet that consisted mainly of seeds, roots, and berries—a diet typical of modern-day primates—and were compelled to become hunters only as a result of environmental changes which reduced this food supply. Conventional images of the resulting hunter-gatherer societies, however, overemphasize the importance of hunting, which in truth only provided the occasional meal to supplement the plant food gathered on a daily basis. The development of horticulture, which allowed people to stay in one place and invest the effort once expended on looking for food on growing it instead, allowed humankind to rely on a diet wholly based on plant foods. Poverty was obviously one reason for the reliance on such a diet, but over the centuries the most overwhelming reason has been a religious one. The ancient religions of the East and sections of the Buddhist and Hindu faiths, for instance, consider all animal life to be sacred, and followers therefore abstain from eating any flesh. This is no outmoded custom, however. Today, in India, around 70 percent of the population are vegetarian for religious reasons. Sectors of the Christian church also adopted vegetarianism and played a vital role in the early beginnings of the movement on both sides of the Atlantic. Also, despite the declining part religion plays in our everyday lives in the West, it has undoubtedly influenced many of the ethical and moral questions raised by our highly-intensive system of meat production.

Whereas many people in the developing world are vegetarian for reasons of poverty or religion, the vast majority of those adopting a vegetarian diet in the West do so for very different reasons. To those who take a global view, one of the most compelling reasons is the sheer inefficiency of intensive meat production in a world where many go hungry—the huge swathes of land needed for beef production could be given over to crops, which are less ruinous to the environment and make vastly more efficient use of the land. More personal and less difficult than the complexities of world hunger and food supply is the concern for animal welfare. Many people are rightly worried by the way animals are raised and slaughtered, and they refrain from eating meat out of compassion. As if these reasons were not compelling enough, over recent years a meat-free diet has been shown to have substantial health benefits, including a reduced risk of high blood pressure, heart disease, cancer, and diabetes. And these are just the most widely publicized health benefits; there are many others.

In a society whose diet has for centuries been dominated by meat, it is all too easy to forget that a large percentage of the world's inhabitants have a diet that consists largely of vegetable foods. This fact is also disguised by the tendency of foreign restaurants to ignore authentic recipes and tailor their menus to perceived Western tastes by adding meat. This gives a misleading picture of some of our favorite cuisines, and it comes as a surprise to many to discover just how suitable many authentic styles of cooking are for vegetarians. Notable among these are Chinese, Indian, and Mediterranean, which all feature numerous exciting and delicious meat-free recipes.

Yet these are just a few of the styles of cooking that you will find within these pages. Drawing on a myriad recipes from places as far flung as Cuba, North Africa, Eastern Europe, and Thailand, we take you on a culinary tour that highlights some of the world's best and most well-known vegetarian recipes—as well as many with which you will be unfamiliar.

The joy of exploring vegetarian cooking from around the world would once have been limited to the lucky and hardy few who traveled far afield. Today, however, we are in the enviable position of having a vast array of ingredients from around the world at our disposal. The most visible result of this are the rows of colorful and exotic fruits and vegetables in our supermarkets; but fresh produce is just part of the story—sun-dried tomatoes, harissa, and balsamic vinegar are just a few of the exciting flavors to emerge recently, and they are just as valuable to the vegetarian cook as any other. This extraordinarily diverse array of foods offers the cook a unique opportunity to sample the best vegetarian recipes from around the world. Dishes that up until very recently would have been impossible to reproduce outside their country of origin, can now be created in your own kitchen.

The recipes that follow give a taste of some of the world's best vegetarian cooking. Simply turn the pages and you will find yourself on a culinary journey that will provide inspiration for years to come.

APPETIZERS & SNACKS

As the introduction to a meal, an appetizer plays a vital role in
enlivening the tastebuds and setting the style for the meal to follow.
The varied recipes in this chapter have been chosen not only for
their quality, but also to ensure a smooth transition to the featured
main courses. Green Bell Pepper and Avocado Dip, for instance, is
the perfect introduction to a Mexican-themed meal, while Artichauts
Aioli provides an impressive prelude to European recipes. Mixing
and matching styles is also great fun, so why not try Asian Salad and
then jump continents to the Americas for your main course. Also
included in this chapter are a number of snacks, including favorites
such as Falafel, and Spinach and Cheese Pie, as well as unusual
dishes such as Imam Bayildi. What they all have in common,
however, is an evocative and delicious flavor.

Makes 18 Samosas

Vegetable Samosas

AS THE MAJORITY OF THE INDIAN POPULATION IS VEGETARIAN, IT IS HARDLY
SURPRISING THAT THE ORIGINAL RECIPE FOR SAMOSAS IS A VEGETARIAN ONE.

Ingredients

Dough

2 cups all-purpose flour

4 tbsps butter

½ tsp salt

¼ cup warm water

Filling

3 potatoes

2 tbsps cooking oil

½ tsp black or white mustard seeds

1 tsp cumin seeds

2 dried red chilies,
coarsely chopped

1 onion, finely chopped

1-2 fresh green chilies, coarsely
chopped and seeded if a mild
flavor is preferred

½ tsp ground turmeric

1 tsp ground coriander

1 tsp ground cumin

1 tsp salt or to taste

1 tbsp chopped fresh
cilantro leaves

1. Boil the potatoes in their skins while
preparing the dough.

2. To make the dough, add the butter and
salt to the flour and rub in well. Mix to
a soft dough with the water. Knead
until the dough feels soft and velvety.

3. Divide the dough into 9 balls. Rotate
each ball between your palms, then
press it down to make a flat cake. Roll
each cake into a 4-inch circle and cut
into two. Use each semicircle of dough
as one envelope. Set aside while
preparing the filling.

4. When the potatoes are cooked, let them
cool, then peel and dice them, and set
them aside.

5. Heat the 2 tbsps oil in a large skillet and
add the mustard seeds. As soon as they
start crackling, add the cumin seeds, red
chilies, onion, and green chilies. Fry until
the onions are soft. Add the turmeric,
ground coriander, and cumin. Stir
quickly, then add the potatoes and salt.
Reduce heat to low, stir and cook until
the potatoes are thoroughly mixed with
the spices.

6. Remove from the heat and stir in the
cilantro. Cool thoroughly before filling
the samosas. To fill the samosas, moisten
the straight edge of the dough with a
little warm water, fold in half to make a
triangular cone and press the edges
together firmly.

7. Fill the cones with the filling, leaving
about a ¼-inch border at the top.
Moisten the top edges and press together
well. Deep fry the samosas over gentle
heat until they are golden brown. Drain
on paper towels and serve.

TIME Preparation takes about 60 minutes
and cooking also takes about 60 minutes.

Serves 4

Imam Bayildi

THE NAME OF THIS TURKISH DISH MEANS THE IMAM OR PRIEST HAS FAINTED.
APPARENTLY THE DISH WAS SO DELICIOUS THAT HE FAINTED WITH PLEASURE.

Ingredients

2 large eggplants

⅔ cup olive oil

2 onions, finely chopped

2 cloves garlic, minced

2 cups tomatoes, peeled
and chopped

½ tsp allspice

Juice of ½ lemon

1 tsp brown sugar

1 tbsp chopped fresh parsley

1 tbsp pine kernels

Salt and freshly ground
black pepper

1. Cut the eggplants in half lengthwise and scoop out the flesh with a sharp knife, leaving a substantial shell so they do not disintegrate when cooked.

2. Heat half the oil in a saucepan, add the onion and garlic, and fry until the onion has just softened. Add the scooped out eggplant flesh, tomatoes, allspice, lemon juice, sugar, parsley, pine kernels, and a little salt and pepper. Simmer for about 20 minutes until the mixture has thickened.

3. Spoon the filling into the eggplant halves. Place the filled halves side by side in a greased ovenproof dish.

4. Mix the remaining oil with ⅔ cup water and a little salt and pepper. Pour around the eggplants and bake in a preheated 350°F oven for 30 to 40 minutes, or until completely tender.

TIME Preparation takes 25 minutes and cooking takes 1 hour.

SERVING IDEA Serve hot or cold garnished with fresh herbs and accompanied by chunks of whole-wheat bread. If serving cold, chill for at least 2 hours before serving.

Serves 4

Tomato and Mozzarella

THE CLASSIC ITALIAN SUMMER APPETIZER. USE LARGE, JUICY TOMATOES, FRESH
BASIL, MOIST MOZZARELLA, AND THE FINEST OLIVE OIL YOU CAN BUY.

Ingredients

4 large tomatoes

1 package round mozzarella
cheese

10 fresh basil leaves

1 tbsp white wine vinegar

3 tbsps olive oil

Salt and freshly ground
black pepper

1. Cut the mozzarella cheese into rounds. Then, using a pastry cutter, trim the rounds into neat circles.

2. Turn the tomatoes on their sides and cut into neat slices. Discard the small outer slices. Alternate the tomato and mozzarella slices on the serving plates to make an attractive circle.

3. Cut the basil leaves lengthwise into thin strips and mix into the vinegar and olive oil. Season the dressing to taste with salt and pepper and pour over the salad before serving.

TIME Preparation takes about 15 minutes.

COOK'S TIP Use a sharp, finely serrated knife to cut the cheese. Do not push down hard, but use a sawing action; this will keep the slices in one piece.

Tomatoes *Tomatoes have a fascinating history. They originated in South America (the word tomato is derived from an ancient Mexican word, tomatl) with Peru in particular thought to be one of the earliest countries to cultivate it. The popularity of the tomato spread as a result of Spanish and Portuguese explorers returning to Europe with the plant. Initially it was more popular in southern Europe, hence its widespread use around the Mediterranean.*

Serves 4

Cheese and Vine Leaves

IN THIS GREEK RECIPE THE CHEESE IS GRILLED OVER COALS TO GIVE
EXTRA FLAVOR, BUT IT CAN ALSO BE GENTLY BROILED.

Ingredients

*4 large pieces goat's, feta,
or haloumi cheese*

1 cup olive oil

*4 tbsps chopped fresh herbs
such as basil, tarragon,
oregano, marjoram,
and parsley*

1 bay leaf

2 cloves garlic, minced

Squeeze of lemon juice

To serve

*4 fresh vine leaves, washed,
or 4 brine-packed leaves,
soaked 30 minutes*

1 head radicchio

*8 leaves curly endive,
washed and torn into
bite-size pieces*

1. If using goat's cheese, make sure it is not too ripe. Lightly score the surface of whichever cheese is used. Mix together the oil, herbs, garlic, and lemon juice.

2. Place the cheese in a small, deep bowl or jar and pour over the oil mixture. If cheese is not completely covered, pour on more oil. Cover and leave in the refrigerator overnight.

3. Drain the cheese and place in a hinged wire rack. Grill the cheese over hot coals until light golden brown and just beginning to melt.

4. Drain and dry the vine leaves, reserving the oil. Wash the radicchio and separate the leaves. Arrange the radicchio and endive leaves on 4 small plates and place a vine leaf on top. Place the cooked cheese on top of the vine leaf and spoon some of the oil mixture over each serving.

TIME Overnight soaking is required for the cheese. Cooking takes 4 to 5 minutes.

Serves 3 – 4

Eggplant Slices in Yogurt

VARIATIONS OF THIS DELICIOUS INDIAN RECIPE CAN BE FOUND IN
MANY OTHER AREAS, PARTICULARLY TURKEY AND NORTH AFRICA.

Ingredients

1 tsp chili powder

½ tsp ground turmeric

1 large eggplant, cut into
¼-inch thick round slices

Vegetable or olive oil for
deep frying

1¼ cups plain yogurt

1 tsp garam masala

¼ tsp salt

1 green chili, seeded
and chopped

1 tsp chopped fresh
cilantro leaves

1. Rub the chili and turmeric powders into the eggplant slices.

2. Heat the oil in a large pan and deep-fry the eggplant slices, a few at a time, for 2 to 3 minutes. Drain the slices on paper towels.

3. Beat the yogurt and add the garam masala, salt, green chili, and fresh cilantro. Mix well.

4. Arrange the eggplant slices on a serving platter or on individual dishes and pour the yogurt over.

VARIATION For a Middle Eastern flavor leave out the chili powder, turmeric, and garam masala, fry the eggplant with a little garlic and replace the fresh cilantro with mint.

TIME Preparation takes 10 minutes and cooking 10 to 15 minutes.

Cilantro This aromatic herb is a member of
the parsley family, although its taste is very different
from that of its more common relative. Fresh cilantro can
be grown easily and quickly, and is widely used in Asian
cooking (with the exception of Japanese cuisine). In India,
it is often stirred through a curry just before serving to add
extra flavor, whereas in China it is more commonly used as a garnish.

Serves 4

Spinach-stuffed Mushrooms

MUSHROOM RECIPES ARE PARTICULARLY POPULAR IN EUROPEAN COUNTRIES
WHERE THE AGE-OLD TRADITION OF MUSHROOM GATHERING HAS SURVIVED.

Ingredients

4 large or 8 medium flat
mushrooms, stalks discarded

¼ cup butter

4 cloves garlic, minced

2 onions, finely chopped

½ tsp nutmeg

1 tbsp olive oil

8 ounces spinach, trimmed,
cooked, and finely chopped

2 tbsps fresh white bread crumbs

Salt and freshly ground
black pepper

1 egg, beaten

1 tbsp chopped fresh parsley
to garnish

1. Heat the butter in a skillet. Add garlic, onion, and nutmeg, and fry gently until the onion has softened. Remove from the pan and set aside to cool.

2. Heat the oil in the skillet and sauté the mushrooms on both sides until lightly browned. Place underside-up in a shallow, ovenproof dish. Mix together the onion mixture, spinach, bread crumbs, and salt and pepper to taste. Stir in the beaten egg.

3. Cover each mushroom cap with the mixture, shaping neatly. Cover with aluminum foil and bake in a preheated 400°F oven for 10 minutes. Serve immediately, garnished with chopped parsley.

TIME Preparation takes 15 minutes and cooking takes 20 minutes.

Mushrooms *It is estimated that there are thousands of edible varieties of mushroom in existence around the world, only a small percentage of which are harvested. The common mushroom is the most widely available in the West, although unusual varieties such as ceps and morels are becoming more widely available, as is the delicious range of Oriental mushrooms, in particular shittakes.*

Serves 4

Green Bell Pepper and Avocado Dip

THAT FAVORITE MEXICAN SNACK GUACAMOLE IS EXPANDED UPON IN THIS RECIPE.
MEXICAN AVOCADOS ARE GENERALLY REGARDED AS THE BEST, SO LOOK OUT FOR THEM.

Ingredients

2 green bell peppers,
halved and cored

½ small fresh green chili,
finely chopped

1 small avocado

2 garlic cloves, minced

3 green onions, chopped

Finely grated rind and juice
of 1 lime

4 tbsps chopped fresh
cilantro leaves

Salt and freshly ground
black pepper

4 small wheat tortillas,
to serve

Lime wedge and a sprig of
fresh cilantro, to garnish

TIME Preparation takes about
20 minutes and cooking takes 10 minutes.

1. Place the bell peppers, cut sides downward, on a broiler pan. Broil under very high heat for 10 minutes, until blackened. Peel off the skin and chop the flesh.

2. Place the bell peppers and the remaining ingredients in a food processor or blender. Purée until smooth. Check the seasoning and add more lime juice if necessary.

3. Spoon into a serving bowl, then cover and chill. Garnish with lime and cilantro just before serving. Serve with the tortillas and chunks of crisp, raw vegetables.

Green Bell Peppers *The capsicum family,
to which the bell pepper belongs, originated in South America,
but was widely used in various areas of the American continent
before it eventually spread to Europe. The green bell pepper is an
unripe pepper which if left to ripen turns red.*

Serves 6–12

Spinach and Cheese Pie

TRADITIONALLY MADE AT EASTER, THIS CLASSIC GREEK PIE IS NOW ENJOYED
ALL YEAR ROUND. PACKAGED PASTRY MAKES IT SIMPLICITY ITSELF TO PREPARE.

Ingredients

1 pound package phyllo pastry

2 pounds fresh spinach

3 tbsps olive oil

2 onions, finely chopped

3 tbsps chopped fresh dill

3 eggs, lightly beaten

Salt and freshly ground
black pepper

2 cups feta cheese, crumbled

½ cup butter, melted

1. Unfold the pastry on a flat surface and cut it to fit the baking dish to be used. Keep the pastry covered.

2. Tear the stalks off the spinach, wash the leaves well, and shred with a sharp knife.

3. Heat the oil in a large saucepan, add the onion and cook until soft. Add the spinach and stir over a medium heat for about 5 minutes. Turn up the heat to evaporate any moisture.

4. Allow the spinach and onion to cool, then mix in the dill, eggs, salt and pepper, and cheese.

5. Brush some of the melted butter on the bottom and sides of the baking dish. Brush the top sheet of phyllo pastry and place it in the dish. Brush another sheet and place that on top of the first. Repeat to make 8 layers of pastry.

6. Spread the filling over the layers in the bottom of the dish and cover with another 6 or 7 layers of pastry, brushing each layer with melted butter. Brush the top layer well and score the pastry in square or diamond shapes. Do not cut right through the pastry.

7. Sprinkle the top of the pie with water and bake in a preheated 375°F oven for 40 minutes, or until crisp and golden.

8. Leave the pie to stand for about 10 minutes and then cut through to the bottom layer. Lift out the pieces to a serving dish.

PREPARATION The pie can be cooked in advance and reheated for 10 minutes to serve hot.

TIME Preparation takes about 25 minutes and cooking takes about 40 minutes.

Serves 8

Indonesian-style Stuffed Peppers

FOR THIS ADAPTABLE RECIPE YOU CAN SUBSTITUTE PINE NUTS
OR PEANUTS IF YOU DON'T HAVE CASHEWS.

Ingredients

2 tbsps olive oil

1 onion, chopped

1 clove garlic, minced

2 tsps turmeric

1 tsp crushed coriander seed

2 tbsps flaked coconut

1½ cups mushrooms, chopped

¾ cup bulgur wheat

½ cup raisins

1¼ cups water

2-3 tomatoes, peeled and chopped

½ cup cashew nuts

4 small green bell peppers, cored
and cut in half lengthwise

2 tsps lemon juice

Vegetable broth for cooking

1. Heat the oil in a large saucepan, add the onion and garlic, and fry until lightly browned.

2. Add the turmeric, coriander, and coconut, and cook gently for about 2 minutes. Add the mushrooms and bulgur wheat, and cook for another 2 minutes.

3. Add the raisins, water, and tomatoes, and simmer gently for 15 to 20 minutes until the bulgur wheat is cooked.

4. Meanwhile, toast the cashew nuts in a dry frying pan until golden brown, and blanch the bell peppers in boiling water for 3 minutes.

5. Mix the nuts and lemon juice with the rest of the ingredients and fill the bell peppers with the mixture. Place the filled bell peppers in a large ovenproof dish and pour vegetable broth around them. Cook in a preheated 350°F oven for 20 minutes.

TIME Preparation takes 20 minutes and cooking takes about 45 minutes.

Serves 8

Falafel

THE NATIONAL DISH OF BOTH ISRAEL AND EGYPT, FALAFEL IS A COARSE
PASTE OF SPICED CHICK PEAS SHAPED INTO SMALL PIECES AND DEEP-FRIED.

Ingredients

1 cup chick peas, soaked
overnight in water

1 slice white bread, crust
removed

2 cloves garlic, minced

2 tbsps chopped fresh parsley

¼ cup bulgur wheat, rinsed
and drained

½ tsp ground coriander

½ tsp ground cumin

½ tsp cayenne pepper

1 tsp salt

Oil for deep frying

1. Drain the chick peas and rinse in fresh water. Grind them in a food processor or blender, putting them through twice if necessary to make a coarse paste.

2. Soak the bread in water, then squeeze it dry by hand. Chop the bread and mix with the minced garlic and parsley. Add this mixture to the chick peas. Add the bulgur, spices, and salt, and mix well. Leave in the refrigerator for 30 minutes.

3. In a deep-fat fryer, preferably with a frying basket, heat the oil to very hot, about 350°F, or until a cube of bread will brown in 60 seconds. Wet your hands and shape the mixture into small balls about the size of a walnut.

4. Deep-fry the balls a few at a time for 2 to 3 minutes or until golden. Remove with a skimmer and transfer to paper towels to drain. Serve immediately with mixed salad. Falafel are best when eaten very fresh. Do not store.

SERVING IDEA Falafel is eaten as a snack, packed in pita bread with plenty of lettuce, tomato, and cucumber. It is generally accompanied by a hot sauce containing fenugreek, a bitter herb. An alternative sauce can be made by mixing Tabasco, or similar pepper sauce, with tomato sauce.

VARIATION Substitute canned chick peas for the dried variety, but ensure you rinse them well before use.

TIME Preparation takes about 1 hour, plus overnight soaking for the beans. Cooking takes 10 to 15 minutes.

Serves 4

Asian Salad

THE DEMANDS OF EVER MORE ADVENTUROUS CONSUMERS MEANS THAT MANY STORES
NOW STOCK THE SORT OF EXOTIC LEAVES USED IN THIS EASTERN RECIPE.

Ingredients

10 ounces mixed young Asian
greens such as mustard greens,
bok choy, tatsoi, and mizuna

⅓ Chinese (Napa) cabbage,
cut lengthwise

½ cup snow peas, trimmed
and thinly sliced diagonally

⅓ cup brown mushrooms,
very thinly sliced

2 green onions, cut crosswise
into 1-inch strips

½ cup cold boiled rice

1 tsp toasted sesame seeds,
to garnish

Dressing

1¼ cups vegetable broth

2 tbsps finely chopped red onion

½ tsp finely chopped fresh
ginger root

½ tsp chopped lemon grass

3 sprigs flat-leafed parsley

1 tbsp lime juice

½ tsp salt

2 tsps sesame seeds, toasted
and crushed

½ tsp sugar

1 tsp soy sauce

1 tsp sesame oil

1. First prepare the dressing. Place the broth, onion, ginger, lemon grass, parsley, lime juice, and salt in a small saucepan. Bring to a boil, simmer for 5 minutes until reduced, then strain. Place 6 tbsps of the liquid in a blender with the crushed sesame seeds, sugar, soy sauce, and sesame oil and blend.

2. Tear the greens and bok choy stalks into bite-sized pieces. Slice the Chinese cabbage crosswise.

3. Arrange all the greens and vegetables attractively on individual serving plates with a small mound of rice in the center.

4. Spoon the dressing over the top and sprinkle with the sesame seeds.

TIME Preparation takes 15 minutes.

Green Onions *The green onion is simply an onion that has been picked very young, before it has had a chance to form a bulb. It has an ancient history and is known to have existed in Central Asia long before the start of the Christian era. Today, there are a large number of varieties, many of which are only used in their area of origin.*

Orange, Grapefruit, and Mint Salad

FROM THE HEALTH-CONSCIOUS WEST COAST COMES
THE PERFECT LOW-CALORIE APPETIZER.

Ingredients

2 grapefruits

3 oranges

Liquid sweetener to taste (optional)

8 sprigs of mint

TIME Preparation takes about 20 minutes, plus chilling time.

1. Using a serrated knife, cut away the peel and the white parts from the grapefruit and oranges. Carefully cut inside the skin of each segment to remove each section of flesh.

2. Squeeze the membranes over a bowl to extract all the juice. Sweeten the juice with the liquid sweetener, if required.

3. Arrange the orange and grapefruit segments alternately on 4 individual serving dishes.

4. Using a sharp knife, chop 4 sprigs of the mint very finely. Stir the chopped mint into the fruit juice.

5. Carefully spoon the juice over the arranged fruit segments and chill thoroughly. Garnish with a sprig of mint before serving.

PREPARATION Make sure all the white parts are removed from the fruit, as they produce a bitter flavor.

VARIATION Use ruby grapefruits and blood oranges, when available, in place of the normal types of fruit.

Serves 4

Artichauts Aioli

GARLIC MAYONNAISE MAKES THE PERFECT SAUCE FOR
ARTICHOKES IN THIS TYPICALLY PROVENÇAL APPETIZER.

Ingredients

4 globe artichokes

1 slice lemon

1 bay leaf

Pinch of salt

Sauce aioli

2 egg yolks

2 cloves garlic, minced

*Salt and freshly ground
black pepper*

1 cup olive oil

Lemon juice to taste

Chervil leaves to garnish

TIME Preparation takes
30 minutes and cooking takes
about 35 minutes.

1. To prepare the artichokes, break off the stems
   and twist to remove any tough fibers. Trim the
   base so that the artichokes will stand upright.
   Trim the points from all the leaves and wash
   the artichokes well.

2. Bring a large pan of water to a boil with the
   slice of lemon and bay leaf. Add a pinch of
   salt and, when the water is boiling, add the
   artichokes. Simmer for 35 minutes over a
   moderate heat. While the artichokes are
   cooking, prepare the sauce.

3. Beat the egg yolks and garlic with a pinch of
   salt and pepper in a deep bowl, or in a food
   processor or blender. Add the olive oil, a few
   drops at a time, while whisking by hand, or in
   a thin, steady stream with the machine
   running. If preparing the sauce by hand, once
   half the oil is added, the remainder may be
   added in a thin, steady stream. Add lemon
   juice once the sauce becomes very thick.
   When all the oil has been added, adjust the
   seasoning and add more lemon juice to taste.

4. When the artichokes are cooked, the bottom
   leaves will pull away easily. Remove them from
   the water with a draining spoon and drain
   upside down on paper towels or in a colander.
   Allow to cool, and serve with the sauce aioli.
   Garnish with a sprig of chervil.

Serves 4

Hummus

AN AUTHENTIC MIDDLE EASTERN SNACK
THAT HAS GAINED WIDESPREAD POPULARITY.

Ingredients

1 cup cooked or canned chick peas
(reserve liquid)

4 tbsps light tahini (sesame paste)

Juice of 2 lemons

½ cup olive oil

3-4 cloves garlic, minced

Salt to taste

1. Put the chick peas in a food processor or blender together with ⅔ cup of the reserved cooking liquid or can juices.

2. Add the tahini, lemon juice, half of the olive oil, garlic, and salt. Blend until smooth, adding a little more liquid if it is too thick.

3. Leave to stand for an hour or so to let the flavors develop. Serve with the remaining olive oil drizzled over the top.

TIME Preparation takes 10 minutes, standing time is 1 hour.

Artichoke   *The globe artichoke is the flower bud of a member of the thistle family. In addition to its delicious flavor and unusual texture, the globe artichoke has valuable nutritional qualities, including diuretic and purgative properties and a significant amount of vitamin C, folic acid, and iron. Small artichoke heads, which are picked at the end of season, can often be found preserved in olive oil.*

Left: Artichauts Aioli

Serves 6

Burritos

THE NAME OF THIS TEX-MEX RECIPE MEANS "LITTLE DONKEYS."
BEANS ARE THE TRADITIONAL FILLING IN THIS POPULAR DISH.

Ingredients

6 tortillas (see page 124)

1 tbsp oil

1 onion, chopped

1 pound canned refried beans

6 lettuce leaves, shredded

1 cup grated Cheddar cheese

2 tomatoes, sliced

2 tbsps snipped chives

½ cup sour cream

Chopped fresh cilantro leaves

Taco sauce

1 tbsp oil

1 onion, diced

1 green bell pepper, diced

1 red or green chili

½ tsp ground cumin

½ tsp ground coriander

½ clove garlic, minced

Pinch of salt, freshly ground
black pepper, and sugar

14 ounces canned tomatoes

Tomato paste (optional)

1. Wrap the tortillas in foil, and heat in a warm oven to soften.

2. Heat the oil in a large skillet, add the onion, and cook until soft but not colored. Add the beans and heat through.

3. Spoon the mixture down the center of each tortilla. Top with lettuce, cheese, tomatoes, and chives. Fold over the sides to form a long rectangular parcel. Make sure the filling is completely enclosed.

4. Place burritos in an ovenproof dish, cover, and cook in a preheated 350°F oven for about 20 minutes.

5. Meanwhile, make the taco sauce. Heat the oil in a heavy-based saucepan and, when hot, add the onion and bell pepper. Cook slowly to soften slightly.

6. Chop the chili, and add with the cumin, coriander, and garlic. Cook for 2 to 3 minutes, then add the seasoning, sugar, and tomatoes with their juice. Break up the tomatoes with a fork or a potato masher.

7. Cook for another 5 to 6 minutes over moderate heat to reduce and thicken slightly. Add tomato paste for color, if necessary.

8. Spoon the taco sauce over the cooked burritos. Top with sour cream and sprinkle with chopped cilantro to serve.

TIME Preparation takes about 25 minutes, not including making the tortillas. Cooking takes about 30 minutes.

PREPARATION Heat just before serving as Burritos do not reheat well.

SERVING IDEAS Serve with rice and guacamole.

Serves 6 – 8

Gazpacho

THIS TYPICALLY SPANISH SOUP IS THE PERFECT SUMMER FIRST COURSE.
THE RECIPE COMES FROM ANDALUSIA, IN SOUTHERN SPAIN.

Ingredients

1 green bell pepper, cored
and chopped

8 tomatoes, peeled, seeded,
and chopped

1 large cucumber, peeled
and chopped

1 large onion, chopped

3-5 ounces French bread,
crusts removed

3 tbsps red wine vinegar

3 cups water

Pinch of salt and freshly
ground black pepper

2 cloves garlic, minced

3 tbsps olive oil

2 tsps tomato paste (optional)

Garnish

1 small onion, diced

½ small unpeeled cucumber, diced

3 tomatoes, peeled, seeded,
and diced

½ green bell pepper, cored
and diced

1. Combine all the prepared vegetables in
a deep bowl and add the bread,
breaking it into small pieces by hand.
Mix together thoroughly.

2. Add the vinegar, water, salt, pepper,
and garlic. Pour the mixture, a third at a
time, into a food processor or blender
and purée for about 1 minute, or until
the soup is smooth.

3. Pour the purée into a clean bowl and
gradually beat in the olive oil using a
whisk. Add enough tomato paste for a
good red color.

4. Cover the bowl tightly and refrigerate
for at least 2 hours, or until thoroughly
chilled. Before serving, beat the soup to
make sure all the ingredients are
blended, and then pour into a large
chilled soup tureen or into chilled
individual soup bowls. Serve all the
garnishes in separate bowls.

VARIATION Use only enough garlic to
suit your own taste, or omit it altogether.
Vary the garnishing ingredients by using
croutons, chopped green onions, red
onions, and red or yellow bell peppers.

TIME Preparation takes
about 20 minutes, plus at
least 2 hours chilling.

FRESH SALADS

The popularity of salads is booming. The vast array of exciting
and colorful ingredients that now find their way into our
supermarkets from the four corners of the world is at times
astonishing. In this chapter you will find inspiration for turning
those raw ingredients into delicious and innovative dishes.
From the simple, but stunning, Roast Bell Pepper and Basil
Salad from the Mediterranean to the unusual Papaya and Bean
Sprout Salad from the Orient, this section has a diverse range of
dishes designed to appeal to all tastes.
Some of the best classic dishes are also featured, including
the ultimate French salad, Mesclun, and that most valued
of Middle Eastern salads, Tabouleh.

Serves 4

Roast Bell Pepper and Basil Salad

FOR THOSE WHO DON'T LIKE THE AGGRESSIVE TASTE OF RAW PEPPERS, THIS ITALIAN SALAD IS A REVELATION. BROILING THEM ADDS A WONDERFUL SMOKY, MELLOW TASTE.

Ingredients

4 yellow bell peppers, cored and cut in half

4 red bell peppers, cored and cut in half

1 tbsp virgin olive oil

1 tbsp red wine vinegar

Bunch of fresh basil

TIME Preparation and cooking take about 20 minutes.

SERVING IDEA Serve as a first course, or with another salad as a complete meal.

1. Preheat the broiler. Place the bell pepper halves on a broiler pan and broil under high heat. The peppers can also be broiled over a gas flame or barbecue. They will take 2 to 3 minutes to cook.

2. When the skin is wrinkled and blackened in places, quickly transfer the bell peppers to a large plastic bag, and fold the top over. Leave them in the bag to cool.

3. The skin should now peel off very easily. Slice the bell peppers into narrow strips.

4. Arrange the strips on a flat serving platter and sprinkle with the oil and vinegar. Strew basil leaves over the bell peppers and leave to marinate for an hour or so at room temperature. Do not chill, but eat at room temperature.

Serves 6

Curried Chick Pea and Rice Salad

A BLEND OF AROMATIC SPICES BRINGS AN EXOTIC FLAVOR TO THIS RICE SALAD.
SERVE WITH FRESH MULTIGRAIN BREAD ROLLS AND MIXED SALAD LEAVES.

Ingredients

1 cup mixed brown and wild rice

1 tsp olive oil

1 clove garlic, minced

1 tsp ground coriander

1 tsp ground cumin

1 tsp turmeric

½ tsp hot chili powder

⅔ cup fresh tomato juice

2 tbsps red wine vinegar

1 tbsp tomato ketchup

Salt and freshly ground black pepper

1 cup broccoli flowerets

3 tbsps finely chopped fresh parsley

1 tbsp chopped fresh thyme

2 bunches green onions, chopped

2 x 14-ounce cans chick peas, rinsed and drained

¾ cup golden raisins

1. Cook the rice in a large pan of lightly salted, boiling water for about 20 minutes, or according to the package instructions, until the rice is cooked and just tender. Drain thoroughly and keep hot.

2. Meanwhile, make the dressing. Heat the oil in a saucepan, add the garlic and spices, and cook gently for 2 minutes, stirring.

3. Add the tomato juice, vinegar, tomato ketchup, and seasoning, and mix well.

Heat gently, stirring occasionally, until the mixture comes to a boil. Reduce the heat and keep the dressing warm.

4. Cook the broccoli in a pan of lightly salted, boiling water for about 5 minutes, until just tender. Drain thoroughly.

5. Place the cooked rice in a bowl, add the spicy tomato dressing, and stir to mix. Add the cooked broccoli and the remaining ingredients and toss together to mix. Serve the rice salad warm or cold.

TIME Preparation takes 15 minutes and cooking takes 20 minutes.

Garlic *Valued for centuries in the East as a basic seasoning, garlic has become extremely popular in the US over recent years. Supermarkets tend to stock only one type of garlic, although there are many types, ranging from small white bulbs to the large purple-tinged heads and the round, bulb-like garlic from China.*

Mesclun

A MEDIEVAL FRENCH SALAD WITH A PERCENTAGE OF
BITTER LEAVES THAT GIVE IT A DELICIOUS EDGE.

Ingredients

*Choose from a combination
of these ingredients:*

Leaves

Chicory (curly endive)

Lamb's lettuce (mache)

Radicchio

Rocket plant

Romaine lettuce

Boston lettuce

Mustard greens

Escarole

Watercress

Endive

Herbs

Lovage

Basil

Chives

Chervil

Tarragon

Marjoram

Edible marigold petals

Nasturtium buds and flowers

1. Wash your chosen leaves in cold water
   and dry, either with paper towels or a
   clean tea towel.

2. Mix the leaves together and add your
   chosen mix of herbs. Sprinkle your
   favorite dressing over the salad.

TIME Preparation takes about 10 minutes.

VARIATION Spike your favorite dressing
with a minced clove of garlic and a little
grainy mustard, crushed papaya seeds,
or capers.

Salad Greens

*The variety of cultivated
greens now available
makes it easier than ever
to produce the mix of flavors
required for a mesclun. Lettuce has been
cultivated since very early times and was
undoubtedly known to the Greeks and Romans,
although there were far fewer forms than are
cultivated today.*

Left: Mesclun

Serves 4

Tofu Salad

THIS THAI SALAD CAN ALSO BE SERVED HOT. SIMPLY
RETURN THE TOFU TO THE WOK, HEAT THROUGH AND
SERVE IMMEDIATELY.

Ingredients

½ cup oil

1 cup cubed tofu

2 cloves garlic, minced

½ cup broccoli flowerets

½ cup snow peas

1 tbsp soy sauce

1 tsp salted black beans

½ tsp palm sugar

½ cup vegetable broth

½ tsp cornstarch

VARIATION Use smoked tofu for
a different flavor.

1. Heat the oil in a wok and fry the tofu until golden on all sides. Remove with a slotted spoon, set aside to cool, then refrigerate until required.

2. Pour off most of the oil from the wok. Add the garlic and fry until softened. Stir in the broccoli and snow peas, and stir-fry until just tender.

3. Add the soy sauce, black beans, and sugar and fry for 1 minute.

4. Mix a little of the broth with the cornstarch, return this to the remaining broth, then add this to the wok. Cook until the sauce thickens slightly.

5. Transfer to a serving dish and chill until required. To serve, scatter the tofu cubes over the cooked vegetables.

TIME Preparation takes 15 minutes and
cooking takes about 10 minutes.

Serves 4

Carrot Salad with Sesame Dressing

THE CARROTS IN THIS MIDDLE EASTERN DISH ARE COATED
WITH TAHINI, A DELICIOUS SESAME SEED PASTE.

Ingredients

4 large carrots

1 cup raisins

1 cup chopped walnuts

2 tbsps sesame seeds

Dressing

2 tbsps oil

1 tbsp lemon juice

6 tbsps tahini (sesame paste)

6 tbsps warm water

2 tbsps heavy cream

*Salt and freshly ground
black pepper*

1 tbsp sugar

1. Place the carrots in iced water for 1 hour. Dry them and grate coarsely into a bowl. Add the raisins, nuts, and sesame seeds.

2. Mix the dressing ingredients together thoroughly, adding more cream if the dressing appears too thick. If the dressing separates, beat vigorously until it comes together before adding additional cream.

3. Toss with the carrot salad and serve.

TIME Preparation takes about 1 hour.

Nuts *A valuable source of protein, nuts have always played an important part in the vegetarian diet. They are now imported from many areas of the world, but some of the most healthful are familiar ones such as peanuts and walnuts. Thought to be native to central Asia and south-west Europe, the walnut is also grown in California.*

Serves 4

Rice and Nut Salad

THIS REFRESHING SALAD IS HIGH IN PROTEIN FROM THE RICE,
NUTS, AND BEANS, AND VERY LOW IN SATURATED FATS.

Ingredients

2 tbsps olive oil

2 tbsps lemon juice

Salt and freshly ground
black pepper

¾ cup golden raisins

⅓ cup currants

1¼ cups cooked brown rice,
well drained

¾ cup blanched almonds,
chopped

½ cup cashew nuts,
chopped

½ cup shelled walnuts,
chopped

15-ounce can peach slices in
natural juice, drained
and chopped

¼ cucumber, cubed

¼ cup cooked red kidney
beans

1 tbsp chopped, pitted
black olives

1. Put the olive oil, lemon juice, and salt and pepper into a screw-top jar, and shake vigorously until the mixture has thickened.

2. Put the golden raisins and currants into a small bowl and cover with boiling water. Leave to stand for 10 minutes, then drain the fruit.

3. Mix together the rice, nuts, soaked fruit, peaches, cucumber, kidney beans, and olives in a large mixing bowl.

4. Pour the dressing over the salad and mix together thoroughly, ensuring all the ingredients are evenly coated.

TIME Preparation takes about 15 minutes.

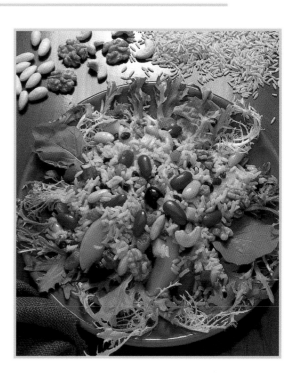

SERVING IDEAS Serve the salad on a bed
of crisp lettuce, or chopped endive.

FRESH SALADS

Serves 4

Pink Grapefruit, Avocado, and Walnuts with Mixed Leaves

THIS CALIFORNIAN-STYLE SALAD IS A LIGHT AND REFRESHING
COMBINATION OF CONTRASTING TEXTURES AND FLAVORS.

Ingredients

1 large red-fleshed grapefruit

1 large avocado

Lemon juice

2 ounces baby spinach leaves,
coarsely shredded

3-4 handfuls frisée lettuce,
torn into bite-sized pieces

Small handful of watercress,
land cress or chia

4 radishes, sliced diagonally

3 tbsps walnut halves

Extra-virgin olive oil

Salt and freshly ground
black pepper

Walnut oil

1. Using a very sharp knife, cut a horizontal slice from the top and the bottom of the grapefruit. Remove the remaining peel and white parts by cutting downward following the contours of the fruit. Working over a bowl, cut down between the flesh and membrane of each segment. Ease out the flesh and put it in a bowl. Cut the segments in half crosswise and set aside with the juice.

2. Cut the avocado in half lengthwise then slice crosswise. Sprinkle with lemon juice.

3. Toss the salad greens with a few drops of olive oil—just enough to barely coat the leaves. Season with salt and freshly ground black pepper. Arrange on individual plates and scatter with the radishes and walnut halves. Add the avocado and grapefruit segments. Sprinkle with the grapefruit juice and just a little dash of the walnut oil, and serve at once.

TIME Preparation takes 15 minutes.

Avocado *The avocado originated in South America, where it has been grown for thousands of years. In contrast, it was virtually unknown in Europe until the second half of the 20th century, when it was introduced by the Israelis. Although it is often said to be high in fat compared to other fruits, it contains monounsaturated fat—the same type so valued in olive oil!*

Serves 4

Black-eyed Bean and Orange Salad

THIS FRENCH-STYLE SALAD HAS A FRESH TASTE THAT IS GIVEN
A DELICIOUS PEPPERY "BITE" BY THE ADDITION OF WATERCRESS.

Ingredients

1½ cups black-eyed beans, soaked

1 bay leaf

1 slice of onion

Juice and grated rind of 1 orange

5 tbsps olive or grapeseed oil

6 black olives, pitted and quartered

4 green onions, trimmed and chopped

2 tbsps each chopped fresh parsley and basil

Salt and freshly ground black pepper

4 whole oranges

1 bunch watercress, washed

1. Place the beans, bay leaf, and onion slice into a saucepan, and add enough water to cover by 1 inch. Bring to a boil and boil rapidly for 10 minutes. Reduce the heat and simmer gently for about 50 minutes to 1 hour, until the beans are tender. Drain well.

2. Put the orange juice, rind, and oil in a large bowl and whisk together with a fork. Stir in the olives, green onions, and chopped herbs.

3. Add the cooked beans to the dressing and season with salt and pepper. Mix thoroughly to coat the beans well.

4. Peel and segment the oranges; chop the segments of 3 of the oranges and add to the beans.

5. Arrange the watercress on individual serving plates and pile equal amounts of the bean and orange salad onto this. Arrange the remaining orange segments on the plate and serve immediately.

SERVING IDEA Serve in split whole-wheat pita bread, or in taco shells.

TIME Preparation takes about 20 minutes, plus soaking. Cooking takes about 1 hour.

Serves 4

Sweet and Sour Mixed-bean Salad

BEANS PROVIDE PROTEIN, FOLIC ACID, IRON, AND POTASSIUM, AND VIRTUALLY NO FAT, ALL
OF WHICH MAKES THEM PERFECT VEGETARIAN FARE.

Dressing

3 tbsps olive oil

3 tbsps unsweetened apple juice

2 tbsps red wine vinegar

2 tbsps clear honey

2 tbsps light soy sauce

2 tbsps tomato ketchup

2 tbsps medium sherry

1 clove garlic, minced

1 tsp ground ginger

Salt and freshly ground
black pepper

1. Steam the green beans over a pan of simmering water for about 10 minutes, until just tender. Drain and rinse under cold water to cool them. Drain well.

2. Place the cooled green beans, onion, bell peppers, raisins, chick peas, corn, kidney beans, and parsley in a large bowl and mix together.

3. Place all the dressing ingredients in a small bowl or blender and whisk together until thoroughly mixed. Pour over the mixed beans and toss together to mix.

TIME Preparation takes 20 minutes and cooking takes 10 minutes.

SERVING IDEA Serve the mixed-bean salad with crusty French bread, or toasted pita pockets.

Ingredients

1¼ cups green beans,
trimmed and halved

1 small Spanish or red onion, sliced

1 small red bell pepper,
cored and diced

1 small yellow bell pepper,
cored and diced

½ cup raisins

14-ounce can chick peas,
rinsed and drained

7-ounce can corn kernels, drained

14-ounce can red kidney beans,
rinsed and drained

2-3 tbsps finely chopped
fresh parsley

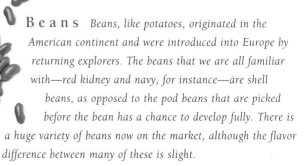

Beans Beans, like potatoes, originated in the American continent and were introduced into Europe by returning explorers. The beans that we are all familiar with—red kidney and navy, for instance—are shell beans, as opposed to the pod beans that are picked before the bean has a chance to develop fully. There is a huge variety of beans now on the market, although the flavor difference between many of these is slight.

Serves 6

Mixed Tomato and Bell Pepper Salad with Parsley Dressing

A FRESH AND COLORFUL MEDITERRANEAN SALAD.

Ingredients

4 red plum tomatoes

4 yellow tomatoes

1 cup cherry tomatoes

1 red bell pepper, cored and
sliced into rings

1 yellow bell pepper, cored and
sliced into rings

1 large Spanish or red onion,
sliced into rings

4 sun-dried tomatoes, soaked,
drained, and finely chopped

Dressing

6 tbsps plain yogurt

4 tbsps mayonnaise

2 tsps wholegrain mustard

3-4 tbsps chopped fresh parsley

Salt and finely ground
black pepper

Fresh parsley sprigs to garnish

1. Slice the plum and yellow tomatoes thinly, and halve the cherry tomatoes.

2. Place the tomatoes, bell peppers, and onion slices in a serving bowl or on a serving platter and toss together to mix. Scatter the sun-dried tomatoes over the top.

3. Place the yogurt, mayonnaise, mustard, parsley, and salt and pepper in a small bowl, and mix thoroughly.

4. Sprinkle the dressing over the tomato-and-pepper salad and toss lightly to mix. Garnish with fresh parsley sprigs before serving.

TIME Preparation takes 15 minutes.

VARIATION Use standard red tomatoes if yellow ones are not available.

*Right: Mixed Tomato and Bell
Pepper Salad with Parsley Dressing*

Moroccan Potato Salad

THIS DELICATELY SPICED POTATO SALAD IS A
GOOD ALTERNATIVE TO THE OFTEN RATHER BLAND
POTATO SALADS OF THE WEST.

Ingredients

2 pounds small new
potatoes, washed

3 tbsps tomato juice

½ tsp ground cumin

½ tsp ground paprika

½ tsp ground coriander

2½ tsps ground turmeric

½ tsp ground cinnamon

½ tsp ground ginger

1 clove garlic, minced
(optional)

2 bunches green onions,
chopped

1 yellow bell pepper, cored
and diced

2-3 tbsps chopped
fresh cilantro

5 tbsps mayonnaise

5 tbsps plain yogurt

Salt and freshly ground
black pepper

1. Cook the potatoes in a large saucepan of lightly salted, boiling water for 10 to 15 minutes, until cooked and tender. Drain thoroughly and allow to cool completely.

2. Place the tomato juice, spices, and garlic, if using, in a small saucepan and cook gently for 2 minutes, stirring. Allow to cool slightly.

3. Place the cold potatoes in a large bowl, add the green onions, yellow bell pepper, and cilantro, and stir to mix.

4. Place the mayonnaise, yogurt, spice mixture, and seasoning in a small bowl and mix together thoroughly. Pour the dressing over the potatoes and toss together to mix.

5. Cover and set aside for 30 minutes before serving. Alternatively, cover and chill in the refrigerator until ready to use.

TIME Preparation takes 20 minutes and cooking takes 20 minutes.

VARIATION This salad may be served warm. Toss the warm cooked potatoes with the dressing and serve.

Serves 4

Tricolor Pasta Salad

THIS SALAD LOOKS ABSOLUTELY STUNNING WITH ITS COLORS OF THE
ITALIAN FLAG. IT IS A FILLING DISH, SUITABLE AS A SUMMER ENTRÉE.

Ingredients

2 cups pasta spirals
(or other pasta shapes)

5 sun-dried tomatoes in oil

⅔ cup vinaigrette dressing
(made with 3 parts virgin
olive oil to 1 part wine vinegar
or lemon juice, plus salt,
pepper, and a pinch of
mustard powder)

5 stems fresh marjoram

3 stems fresh basil

1 cup cubed mozzarella cheese

½ cup black olives, pitted

1. Cook the pasta in plenty of boiling water until al dente—about 12 minutes. Drain the pasta and rinse in plenty of cold water to keep the shapes separate and stop it cooking further. Transfer to a large mixing bowl.

2. Cut the sun-dried tomatoes into small strips. Mix the dressing ingredients, shaking them in a bottle, or blending them in a blender.

3. Snip or mince the marjoram and basil. Combine the cooled pasta with the cheese, olives, and tomatoes. Add enough dressing to lightly coat the pasta, then add the herbs. Stir well, and leave at room temperature, lightly covered, for about 1 hour, for the flavors to combine. Serve at room temperature.

TIME Preparation and cooking take 20 minutes.

SERVING IDEA Serve with Italian breads and a green salad.

Lemon *The original home of the lemon is thought to be southeastern Asia. From there it gradually came west, until in about AD 1000 the Arabs introduced it into the Mediterranean region. To begin with it was only used medicinally, but eventually its culinary importance took precedence. Today, lemons are grown widely in the Mediterranean region, as well as in the United States.*

Serves 4

Warm Salad with Avocado, Grapes, Blue Cheese, and Walnuts

WARM SALADS ARE POPULAR IN FRANCE. THEY ARE UNDOUBTEDLY DELICIOUS, BUT BEWARE—THEY MUST BE SERVED IMMEDIATELY TO PREVENT THE LEAFY INGREDIENTS GOING LIMP.

Ingredients

Mixed salad leaves, such as frisée, chicory, lamb's lettuce, or watercress

2 avocados, peeled and sliced

6 ounces black grapes, halved and pitted

4 tbsps chopped fresh mixed herbs

1 cup walnut pieces

1¼ cups diced or crumbled blue cheese

3 tbsps mixed walnut oil and grapeseed oil

2 tbsps lemon vinegar

Pinch of sugar

1. Tear the salad leaves into small pieces and place in a large bowl. If using lamb's lettuce, separate the leaves and leave whole. Remove any tough stalks from the watercress.

2. Add the avocado slices to the salad leaves, along with the grapes, chopped herbs, walnuts, and cheese.

3. Put the oils, vinegar, and sugar into a screw-topped jar and shake vigorously until the dressing is well blended.

4. Pour the dressing into a large skillet and heat until bubbling. Remove from the heat, add to the prepared salad, and toss, taking care not to break up the avocado pieces. Serve immediately.

TIME Preparation takes about 15 minutes and cooking takes 2 to 3 minutes.

Grapes *Vines are thought to predate mankind's existence and grapes were probably one of the first fruits to be seriously cultivated. The best-known product associated with grapes is of course wine, but they are also widely valued as a fruit, either fresh or dried.*

Serves 4 – 6

Bavarian Potato Salad

IT IS BEST TO PREPARE THIS SALAD A FEW HOURS IN ADVANCE
TO ALLOW THE POTATOES TO ABSORB THE FLAVORS.

Ingredients

2 pounds tiny new potatoes

4 tbsps olive oil

4 green onions, finely chopped

1 clove garlic, minced

2 tbsps chopped fresh dill
or 1 tbsp dried

2 tbsps wine vinegar

½ tsp sugar

Salt and freshly ground
black pepper

2 tbsps chopped fresh
parsley

1. Wash the unpeeled potatoes, put them in a pan, cover with water, and boil until just tender.

2. While the potatoes are cooking, heat the olive oil in a skillet and fry the green onions and garlic for 2 to 3 minutes until they have softened a little. Add the dill and cook gently for another minute.

3. Add the wine vinegar and sugar, and stir until the sugar dissolves. Remove from the heat and add a little salt and pepper.

4. Drain the potatoes and pour the dressing over them while they are still hot. Allow to cool and sprinkle with the chopped parsley before serving.

TIME Preparation takes 15 minutes and cooking takes 15 minutes.

S u g a r *Most widely known as a sweetening agent in desserts, sugar is also valuable for sweetening and balancing the flavor of some savory dishes. Most of the world's refined sugar is derived from sugar cane, a native of the Orient which spread first to the Mediterranean, and then to the American continent in the 16th century.*

Tabouleh

THIS IS A TRADITIONAL SALAD FROM THE MIDDLE EAST. THE MAIN INGREDIENT
IS BULGUR WHEAT, WHICH IS PARTIALLY COOKED CRACKED WHEAT.

Ingredients

¾ cup bulgur wheat

1 tsp salt

1½ cups boiling water

1 pound tomatoes, chopped

½ cucumber, diced

3-4 green onions

Dressing

¼ cup olive oil

¼ cup lemon juice

2 tbsps chopped fresh mint

4 tbsps chopped fresh parsley

2 cloves garlic, minced

1. Mix the bulgur wheat with the salt, pour over the boiling water, and leave to stand for 15 to 20 minutes. All the water will then be absorbed.

2. Mix together the ingredients for the dressing and pour over the soaked bulgur. Fold in lightly with a spoon.

3. Leave for two hours or overnight in a refrigerator or cool place.

4. Add the tomatoes, cucumber, and green onions. Mix together and serve.

COOK'S TIP A few cooked beans can be added to make this dish more substantial.

TIME Preparation takes about 20 minutes; standing time is about 2 hours.

Serves 4

Goat Cheese Salad with Tarragon

THIS MEDITERRANEAN SALAD IS SIMPLICITY ITSELF TO PREPARE. THE FRESH HERBS
AND OLIVE OIL GIVE IT A LOVELY FLAVOR REDOLENT OF SULTRY SUMMER DAYS.

Ingredients

12 small slices white bread

4 small goat cheeses
(not too fresh)

4 small servings of mixed green
salad, washed and dried

1 tbsp chopped fresh tarragon

1 tbsp tarragon vinegar

2 tbsps olive oil

Salt and freshly ground
black pepper

TIME Preparation takes about
25 minutes, and cooking takes
5 minutes.

1. Using a pastry cutter, cut the sliced
bread into 12 neat rounds.

2. Cut each cheese horizontally into
3 rounds the same size as the bread and
place on the prepared bread. Sprinkle
the chopped tarragon over the cheese.

3. To prepare the dressing, mix together
the tarragon vinegar, olive oil, and salt
and pepper. Stir or shake well and pour
over the prepared mixed green salad.

4. Place the cheese and bread rounds into
a moderately hot oven and cook until
the cheese melts slightly and the top is
golden.

5. Remove from the oven and set the
cheese and toast rounds onto the
tossed salad.

Serves 4–6

Oriental Salad

THIS NUTRITIOUS SALAD CONTAINS TOFU. A STAPLE FOOD IN MUCH
OF ASIA, TOFU IS VENERATED FOR ITS HEALTH-GIVING PROPERTIES.

Ingredients

1 cake tofu, cut into small cubes

½ cup vegetable oil

4 ounces snow peas, ends trimmed

¾ cup sliced mushrooms

2 ounces broccoli flowerets

2 carrots, thinly sliced

2 celery sticks, thinly sliced

4 green onions, thinly sliced

½ cup unsalted roasted peanuts

2 cups bean sprouts

½ head Chinese
cabbage, shredded

Dressing

3 tbsps lemon juice

2 tsps honey

1 tsp grated fresh ginger root

3 tbsps soy sauce

Dash of sesame oil

1. Drain the tofu well and press gently to remove excess moisture. Cut into ¼-inch cubes.

2. Heat 2 tbsps from the ½ cup oil in the wok or skillet (save the remaining oil for the dressing).

3. Add the snow peas, mushrooms, broccoli, carrots, and celery, and cook for 2 minutes. Remove the vegetables and set them aside to cool.

4. When cool, mix the cooked vegetables with the onions, peanuts, and bean sprouts. Mix the dressing ingredients together and pour over the vegetables. Add the tofu and toss carefully.

5. Arrange a bed of Chinese cabbage on a serving dish and pile the salad ingredients on top to serve.

TIME Preparation takes 25 minutes, and cooking takes 2 minutes.

Snow Peas *These young pea pods, picked before the peas have matured, have a fresh, crunchy flavor. They are commonly used in two very different styles of cooking, French and Chinese. Where others disdain the humble pea, the French have always treated it with the respect it deserves and have done much to champion snow peas. In Chinese cooking, it is valued for its crunchy texture in stir-fries.*

Serves 6

Curried Rice Salad

ALTHOUGH INFLUENCED BY INDIAN COOKING, THIS RECIPE IS UNDOUBTEDLY
AN AMALGAM OF VARIOUS STYLES. IT IS DELICIOUS NONETHELESS.

Ingredients

¾ cup long-grain rice

1 tbsp curry powder

4 green onions, trimmed
and sliced

2 celery sticks, sliced

1 small green bell pepper, diced

10 black olives, halved and pitted

¼ cup golden raisins

½ cup toasted slivered almonds

4 tbsps flaked coconut

2 hard-cooked eggs, chopped

Dressing

½ cup mayonnaise

1 tbsp mango chutney

Juice and grated rind of ½ lime

4 tbsps plain yogurt

Salt

Garnish

2 avocados, peeled and cut
into cubes

Juice of ½ lime or lemon

1. Cook the rice in boiling, salted water for about 12 minutes, or until tender. During the last 3 minutes of cooking time, drain away half the water and stir in the curry powder. Leave to continue cooking over a gentle heat until the rice is cooked and the water has evaporated.

2. Leave to stand, covered, for about 5 minutes. Toss the rice with a fork, drain away any excess water, and leave to cool.

3. Combine the rice with the remaining salad ingredients, stirring carefully so that the eggs do not break up.

4. Mix the dressing ingredients together thoroughly. Chop any large pieces of mango in the chutney finely. Stir the dressing into the salad and toss gently to coat.

5. Arrange the rice salad in a mound on a serving dish. Sprinkle the cubed avocado with the lemon juice to keep it green and place around the rice salad before serving.

TIME Preparation takes 20 minutes and cooking takes about 12 minutes.

Lime *Limes are thought to be native to southern Asia and were introduced to the Middle East and the Mediterranean by the Arabs in the 10th century. Today, they are cultivated all over the subtropical world, with the West Indies and Mexico being the world's principal suppliers.*

Serves 4

Greek Salad

A GREAT FAVORITE THAT HAS THE ADDED
ADVANTAGE OF BEING EASY TO PREPARE.

Ingredients

2 tomatoes

½ green bell pepper, cored and
coarsely chopped

¼ cucumber, coarsely chopped

2 celery sticks, finely sliced

1 tsp finely chopped fresh basil

Few crisp leaves of lettuce

1 cup diced feta cheese

16 black olives, pitted

Dressing

4 tbsps olive oil

2 tbsps lemon juice

1 clove garlic, minced

Large pinch of oregano

Salt and freshly ground
black pepper

1. Cut each tomato into eight pieces and
put into a large mixing bowl. Add the
bell pepper, cucumber, celery, and
chopped basil.

2. Mix together the oil, lemon juice, garlic,
oregano, and salt and pepper, and pour
over the salad. Mix well to coat all the
vegetables.

3. Arrange a few leaves of lettuce in the
bottom of a serving bowl and pile the
salad on the top, followed by the
cheese cubes. Garnish with the olives.

TIME Preparation takes 15 minutes.

Lettuce *This invaluable salad ingredient has been
grown for thousands of years, first by the Chinese and later
by the Greeks and Romans, who did much to spread its use
throughout Europe. In contrast to the way it is commonly served
today, during the Middle Ages lettuce was braised and served hot.*

Serves 2

Papaya and Bean Sprout Salad

BEAN SPROUTS AND PAPAYA ADD A TASTE OF THE ORIENT
TO THIS REFRESHING SALAD.

Ingredients

1 large, ripe papaya

Squeeze of lime juice

7 ounces (about 4 handfuls)
green and red salad leaves
such as frisée, romaine, lamb's
lettuce, and oakleaf lettuce, torn
into bite-sized pieces

½ ounce (small handful)
arugula

½ small cucumber,
very thinly sliced

½ cup bean sprouts

Citrus dressing

¼ tsp Dijon mustard

1 tsp olive oil

1½ tbsps orange juice

1½ tbsps fresh lime juice

Pinch of sugar

Salt and freshly ground
black pepper to taste

TIME Preparation takes
15 minutes.

1. Halve the papaya lengthwise and scoop
out the seeds, reserving a few for
garnish. Using a small, sharp knife,
carefully remove the skin. Slice the flesh
lengthwise into thin segments. Place in
a shallow dish and sprinkle with a
squeeze of lime juice.

2. Arrange the leaves on individual plates.
Scatter the cucumber, bean sprouts,
and papaya over the top, and sprinkle
with the reserved papaya seeds.

3. Purée the dressing ingredients in a
blender and spoon over the salad. Serve
at once with crackers or crusty bread.

Serves 6

Pasta and Vegetables in Parmesan Dressing

THIS WONDERFUL PASTA SALAD IS BOTH COLORFUL AND DELICIOUS.

Ingredients

1 pound pasta spirals or other shapes

8 ounces assorted vegetables such as:

Zucchini, cut into rounds or julienne strips

Broccoli, trimmed into very small flowerets

Snow peas, ends trimmed

Carrots, cut into julienne

Celery, cut into julienne

Cucumber, cut into julienne

Green onions, thinly shredded or sliced

Asparagus tips

French beans, sliced

Red or yellow bell peppers, cored and thinly sliced

Dressing

½ cup olive oil

3 tbsps lemon juice

1 tbsp chopped fresh parsley

1 tbsp chopped fresh basil

½ cup freshly grated Parmesan cheese

2 tbsps mild mustard

Salt and freshly ground black pepper

Pinch of sugar

1. Cook pasta in a large saucepan of boiling, salted water with 1 tbsp oil for 10 to 12 minutes, until just tender. Rinse under hot water to remove starch. Leave in cold water.

2. Place all the vegetables, except the cucumber, into boiling, salted water for about 3 minutes, until just tender. Rinse in cold water and leave to drain.

3. Mix the dressing ingredients together well.

4. Drain the pasta thoroughly and toss with the dressing. Add the vegetables and toss to coat.

TIME Preparation takes 25 minutes and cooking takes about 15 minutes.

Asparagus The asparagus sold in supermarkets is a cultivated variety of a type that can still be found growing wild around the Mediterranean and in western and central Asia. There are three main varieties of asparagus: white, purple, and green. White asparagus is picked as soon as the spears of the plant appear through the soil, the purple is harvested when the shoots are a little higher, and the green when they are higher still.

Serves 4

Quinoa Salad

THIS LIGHT SALAD USES QUINOA, THE SOUTH
AMERICAN SEED THAT THE INCAS ONCE REFERRED TO
AS "THE MOTHER GRAIN." IT CONTAINS A HIGH
AMOUNT OF PROTEIN AND HAS A DELICATE, SLIGHTLY
NUTTY FLAVOR.

Ingredients

¾ cup quinoa

Seeds from 4 cardamom pods,
crushed

2 cups water

Salt

1 tsp tamari (Japanese soy sauce)

2 tsps olive oil

Freshly ground black pepper

⅔ cup trimmed snow peas

¼ cup halved seedless
black grapes

3 tbsps snipped chives

Radicchio and Bibb lettuce

TIME Preparation takes
20 minutes and cooking takes
15 minutes plus standing.

VARIATION Use bulgur wheat
instead of quinoa.

1. Dry-fry the quinoa and cardamom
   seeds in a small saucepan for a minute
   or two, until the quinoa starts to color.

2. Add the water and ½ tsp salt. Bring to
   a boil, cover and simmer over very low
   heat until the liquid is absorbed, about
   15 minutes.

3. Remove from the heat, fluff up with a
   fork, and stir in the lemon juice,
   tamari, and olive oil. Transfer to a bowl
   and leave to cool.

4. Plunge the snow peas into boiling
   water for 30 seconds, then drain. Slice
   diagonally into three, and stir into the
   quinoa.

5. Set aside a few grapes as a garnish, and
   add the remainder to the quinoa. Stir in
   the chives and salt and pepper to taste.

6. When ready to serve, arrange the
   lettuce leaves around the edge of a
   shallow serving dish or individual
   plates, and pile the quinoa salad on
   top. Garnish with the reserved grapes
   and serve with crackers.

Left: Quinoa Salad

S e r v e s   4 – 6

Sweet and Sour Fruit Salad

DON'T BE PUT OFF BY THE SAVORY SEASONING IN THIS EXOTIC SALAD—IT GIVES THE DISH A DEFINITE EDGE. SERVE AS AN APPETIZER, SIDE SALAD, OR SNACK.

Ingredients

2 bananas, peeled and sliced

1 large guava, chopped

1 pear, peeled and chopped

8-10 ounces canned peaches, drained and chopped

8-10 ounces canned pineapple chunks, drained

1 small, fresh papaya, peeled, seeded and cut into chunks

A few grapes, seeded

1 apple, peeled, cored and chopped

2 tsps lemon juice

Salt

¼ tsp freshly ground black pepper

¼ tsp chili powder

Pinch of black rock salt (kala namak)

1. Put all the fruits into a large bowl. Sprinkle with lemon juice, salt, pepper, and chili. Mix well.

2. Add pinch of ground black rock salt. Mix and serve. Note: many other fruits may be added, such as mango, kiwi, plum, litchis, melons, etc.

TIME Preparation takes 20 to 25 minutes.

Pears *The first pears were the small, green fruits of the wild pear tree, which can still be found growing all over Europe and as far east as the Himalayas. By Roman times, Pliny, that tireless compiler of botanical information, could list 38 varieties. Today there are over 3000, although only a few are cultivated widely.*

MAIN MEALS

The main course is usually the focal point of a meal and as such it needs to be inspired, delicious, and nutritious. Drawing on classic and innovative recipes from around the world, this chapter fulfills these criteria by embracing the lighter, brighter colors and textures that are so popular today.

The inhabitants of many exotic countries have long understood how to cook vegetables—stir-frying is a perfect example—and this is reflected in their cuisines. With everything from classic Chinese stir-fries to a Herbed Lentil Stew, Tunisian Couscous from the Middle East, and Gado Gado from Indonesia, this chapter reflects the diversity that makes vegetarian cooking across the world so exciting.

Serves 4

Ten Varieties of Beauty

THE NUMBER "TEN" REFERS TO THE SELECTION OF VEGETABLES IN THIS
EXOTIC CHINESE DISH, WHICH IS SIMPLICITY ITSELF TO MAKE.

Ingredients

10 dried Shittake mushrooms

2 carrots

4 tbsps vegetable oil

3 celery sticks, trimmed and
sliced diagonally

3 ounces snow peas

8 baby corn cobs, halved
lengthwise

1 red bell pepper, cored
and sliced

4 green onions, sliced

1 cup bean sprouts

10 water chestnuts, sliced

2-ounce can sliced bamboo
shoots, drained

⅔ cup vegetable broth

2 tbsps cornstarch

3 tbsps light soy sauce

1 tsp sesame oil

1. Place the mushrooms in a bowl and add boiling water to cover. Leave to stand for 30 minutes. Drain the mushrooms, and remove and discard the stalks.

2. Cut the carrots into ribbons using a potato peeler.

3. Heat the oil in a wok or large skillet, add the celery, snow peas, and baby corn, and fry for 3 minutes. Add the bell pepper and carrots and stir-fry for 2 minutes.

4. Stir in the remaining vegetables and stir-fry for 3 to 4 minutes, until all the vegetables are cooked, but still crisp.

5. Add the broth to the pan. Combine the cornstarch, soy sauce, and sesame oil, and stir into the pan. Cook, stirring constantly, until the sauce thickens. Serve immediately.

TIME Preparation takes 15 minutes, plus soaking. Cooking takes about 15 minutes.

Serves 4

Chick Pea and Bell Pepper Casserole

CHICK PEAS ARE USED EXTENSIVELY IN MIDDLE EASTERN CUISINE. HERE, GROUND
CUMIN AND MINT GIVE THIS COLORFUL CASSEROLE A REAL NORTH AFRICAN FLAVOR.

Ingredients

1⅓ cups chick peas, soaked
overnight

2 tbsps vegetable oil

1 onion, sliced

1 clove garlic, minced

1 green bell pepper, cored
and sliced

1 red bell pepper, cored
and sliced

½ tsp ground cumin

2 tsps chopped fresh parsley

1 tsp chopped fresh mint

4 medium tomatoes, seeded
and cut into strips

Salt and freshly ground
black pepper

TIME Preparation takes 20 minutes, plus
overnight soaking. Cooking takes about
3 hours.

1. Drain the chick peas, rinse, and place in
a pan with enough water to cover them
by 1 inch. Bring to a boil and boil
rapidly for 10 minutes. Reduce the heat
and simmer gently for about 2 hours, or
until the chick peas are soft. Drain and
reserve the liquid.

2. Heat the oil in a saucepan and fry the
onion, garlic, and bell peppers for
5 minutes. Stir in the cumin and fry
for 1 minute.

3. Make the reserved liquid up to 1¼ cups
and add to the pan with the cooked
beans.

4. Add all the remaining ingredients and
bring slowly to a boil. Cover and
simmer for 30 minutes. Adjust the
seasoning, if necessary, and serve.

Serves 4

Whole-wheat Vegetable Quiche

QUICHES ARE A GREAT FAVORITE IN BRITAIN AND FRANCE; THIS RECIPE IS UNUSUAL IN THAT IT HAS A WHOLE-WHEAT CRUST.

Ingredients

Generous 1 cup whole-wheat all-purpose flour

6 tbsps vegetable margarine

About 2 tbsps cold water

2 tbsps oil

1 small red bell pepper, cored and diced

1 zucchini, diced

2 green onions, trimmed and sliced

1 tomato, peeled, seeded, and chopped

2 eggs, beaten

⅔ cup milk

Salt and freshly ground black pepper

Tomato slices and chopped fresh parsley to garnish

1. Place the flour in a bowl and rub in the margarine until the mixture resembles fine bread crumbs. Add enough cold water to mix to a firm dough, then roll out and use to line an 8-inch tart pan.

2. Line the pie shell with baking parchment and fill with baking beans. Bake for 15 minutes in a preheated 400°F oven, removing the parchment and beans halfway through the cooking time.

3. Reduce the oven temperature to 350°F. Heat the oil in a small pan and fry the bell pepper and zucchini for 2 minutes. Add the green onion and tomato and fry for 1 minute. Spoon the vegetable mixture into the flan case.

4. Beat the eggs and milk together and season well. Pour over the vegetables. Return to the oven and bake for 30 minutes, or until the filling is just set. Garnish with sliced tomatoes and chopped parsley.

TIME Preparation takes about 15 minutes and cooking takes about 50 minutes.

Pepper *Both black and white peppercorns come from a vine of the* Peperaceae *family, which grows widely in southeast Asia. Black peppercorns come from the unripe berries, which are fermented and dried until they blacken and become hard. White pepper, in contrast, is made by sun-drying the inner seed of the peppercorn.*

Serves 4–6

Mixed Vegetable Curry

IN THIS INDIAN CURRY, A VARIETY OF SEASONAL VEGETABLES ARE COOKED
TOGETHER IN A SAUCE FLAVORED BY GROUND SPICES, ONIONS, AND TOMATOES.

Ingredients

4-5 tbsps vegetable oil

1 large onion, finely chopped

½-inch cube fresh ginger root,
peeled and finely sliced

1 tsp ground turmeric

1 tsp ground coriander

1 tsp ground cumin

1 tsp paprika

4 small ripe tomatoes,
peeled and chopped

2 small potatoes, peeled
and diced

½ cup sliced green beans

¾ cup sliced carrots

½ cup shelled peas

Scant 2 cups warm water

2-4 whole fresh green chilies

1 tsp garam masala

1 tsp salt, or to taste

1 tbsp chopped fresh
cilantro leaves

1. Heat the oil over medium heat, add the onion and fry until lightly browned, about 6 to 7 minutes.

2. Add the ginger root and fry for 30 seconds. Adjust heat to low and add the turmeric, coriander, cumin, and paprika. Stir to mix well. Add half the tomatoes and fry for 2 minutes, stirring continuously.

3. Add the potatoes, green beans, carrots, peas, and water. Stir well. Bring to a boil, cover, and simmer until vegetables are tender, about 15 to 20 minutes.

4. Add the remaining tomatoes and the chilies. Cover and simmer for 5 to 6 minutes.

5. Add the garam masala and salt, and mix well. Stir in half the cilantro leaves and remove from the heat. Put the curry into a serving dish and sprinkle the remaining cilantro leaves on top.

COOK'S TIP Frozen peas and beans may be used for convenience, but the cooking time should be adjusted accordingly.

TIME Preparation takes 25 to 30 minutes and cooking takes 30 minutes.

Tunisian Couscous

COUSCOUS IS A TYPE OF FINE SEMOLINA MADE FROM WHEAT GRAIN. IT IS
STEAMED OVER A STEW OR BROTH WHICH IT IS THEN MIXED THROUGH.

Ingredients

3 cups strong vegetable broth

1 onion, coarsely chopped

2 garlic cloves, minced

1 tsp cumin seeds, toasted and crushed

1 cup peeled, chopped tomatoes

4 carrots, quartered

1 small celery root, cut into 1-inch pieces

4 potatoes, quartered

½ tsp harissa or chili powder

½ tsp salt

¼ tsp freshly ground black pepper

2½ cups couscous

3 zucchini, cut into 1-inch slices

Chopped fresh cilantro to garnish

1. Heat 6 tbsps of the broth in a large pan over which a steamer will fit. Add the onion and cook over medium heat until soft.

2. Add the garlic, cumin, and tomatoes, and cook for 2 to 3 minutes, stirring.

3. Add the carrots, celery root, potatoes, remaining broth, harissa or chili, and salt and pepper. Bring to a boil, cover, and simmer for 20 minutes.

4. Soak the couscous in warm water for 10 minutes. Drain thoroughly and put in a metal sieve or cheesecloth-lined steamer.

5. Add the zucchini to the vegetables, then fit the steamer over the pan, making sure the bottom does not touch the stew. Steam the couscous, covered, for 30 minutes, until heated through.

6. To serve, turn the couscous into a shallow serving dish and fluff with a fork. Moisten with a little broth from the vegetables. Using a slotted spoon, arrange the vegetables in the middle and garnish with cilantro. Serve the remaining vegetable broth in a pitcher.

TIME Preparation takes 30 minutes and cooking takes 50 minutes.

COOK'S TIP Ethnic stores sell couscous and the special steamer in which to cook it, known as a couscousière.

SERVING IDEA Serve the couscous with pita bread and a bowl of plain yogurt sprinkled with ground coriander and a pinch of cayenne pepper.

Green Beans These are simply the unripe pods of a standard bean plant. It is thought the bean plant originated in America and was introduced into Europe in the 16th century. It was particularly popular in France, hence its alternative name of French bean.

Serves 4

Ravioli with Ricotta Cheese

MAKING YOUR OWN PASTA GIVES A REAL INSIGHT INTO WHY ITALIANS ENJOY
THE WHOLE PROCESS OF PREPARING AND EATING HOME-COOKED FOOD.

Ingredients

Filling

2 tbsps butter or margarine

1 egg yolk

½ pound ricotta cheese

¼ cup Parmesan cheese, grated

2 tbsps chopped fresh parsley

Salt and freshly ground black pepper

Dough

2 cups bread flour

Pinch of salt

3 eggs

Tomato sauce

1 tbsp olive oil

2 strips bacon

1 small onion, chopped

1 bay leaf

1 tsp dried basil

1 tbsp flour

14 ounces canned tomatoes

Salt and freshly ground black pepper

1 tbsp heavy cream

1. To make the filling, beat the butter to a cream, add the egg yolk, and blend well. Beat the ricotta cheese to a cream and add the butter-egg mixture gradually, mixing until smooth. Add the Parmesan cheese, parsley, and salt and pepper to taste. Set aside.

2. To make the dough, sift the flour in a bowl with the salt. Make a well in the center and add the eggs. Work the flour and eggs together with a spoon, then knead by hand until a smooth dough is formed. Leave to rest for 15 minutes.

3. Lightly flour a board and roll the dough out thinly into a rectangle. Cut the dough in half.

4. Shape the filling into small balls and set them about 1½ inches apart on one half of the dough. Place the other half on top and cut out the ravioli with a small pastry cutter. Seal the edges with a fork or your fingertips.

5. Cook the ravioli in batches in a large, wide pan with plenty of boiling, salted water until tender, about 8 minutes. Remove carefully with a slotted spoon.

6. While the pasta is boiling, prepare the sauce. Heat the oil, add the bacon and onion, and fry until golden. Add the bay leaf and basil, and stir in the flour. Cook for 1 minute, remove from the heat, and add the tomatoes gradually, stirring continuously. Add salt and pepper to taste.

7. Return the pan to the heat and bring to a boil. Simmer for 5 minutes, remove the bay leaf, and press the sauce through a sieve. Stir in the cream and adjust the seasoning.

8. Pour the sauce over the ravioli and serve immediately.

COOK'S TIP Always buy fresh Parmesan and grate it yourself as its flavor is far superior to that of ready-grated Parmesan.

TIME Preparation takes 30 minutes, cooking takes 20 minutes.

Serves 4

Daal Dumplings in Yogurt

TWO TYPES OF DAAL FEATURE IN THIS UNUSUAL AND DELICIOUS INDIAN RECIPE.
MOONG DAAL IS SIMILAR TO YELLOW SPLIT LENTILS, WHILE URID DAAL IS A WHITE LENTIL.

Ingredients

1 cup urid daal, washed and
soaked for 1 hour

½ cup moong daal, washed
and soaked for 1 hour

½ tsp salt

1-inch piece ginger root, peeled
and finely chopped

2 green chilies, finely chopped

4 tbsps mixed raisins and
golden raisins

Vegetable or olive oil for
deep frying

Yogurt sauce

2 cups plain yogurt

¼ tsp salt

½ tsp cumin seeds

½ tsp coriander seeds

2 sprigs fresh cilantro
leaves, chopped
for garnish

1. Blend the drained urid daal and moong daal with sufficient water in a food processor or blender to make a very thick purée. Put the purée into a mixing bowl, add salt, ginger, chilies, and mixed fruits. Mix well.

2. Heat the oil and add small spoonfuls of the mixture to the hot oil to make small dumplings. (To make more uniform dumplings, dampen your hands in water, and form a little mixture into a flat, round shape before lowering the mixture gently into the oil.) Fry for 6 to 8 minutes, or until golden brown, turning occasionally. Drain on paper towels. Make all the dumplings in the same way.

3. Soak the fried dumplings in water for 2 to 3 minutes. Gently squeeze out any excess water and arrange on a flat serving dish. Mix the yogurt and salt together and pour over the dumplings.

4. Dry roast the cumin and coriander seeds for 1 to 2 minutes in a skillet. Place the roasted spices in folded paper towels and crush with a rolling pin to give a coarse powder.

5. Sprinkle the ground spice mixture over the yogurt and garnish with chopped fresh cilantro. Alternatively, sprinkle with a pinch of paprika powder.

TIME Preparation takes 5 minutes and 1 hour for soaking. Cooking takes about 30 minutes.

Ginger Root *Originating in India, fresh ginger root is widely used in Oriental cooking. Having spread to Europe, ginger was then taken by the Spanish to the West Indies, from where its cultivation spread rapidly. As well as being used fresh, ginger root is also pickled (when it turns a light pink color) and used as a garnish in China and Japan.*

Makes One Pizza

Roast Eggplant and Tomato Pizza

DESPITE ITS OVEREXPOSURE, PIZZA REMAINS A GREAT BOON FOR VEGETARIANS.
THIS RECIPE IS JUST THAT LITTLE BIT DIFFERENT.

Ingredients

Dough

2 cups all-purpose flour

Pinch of salt

¼ ounce package easy-blend
dried yeast

1 tbsp olive oil

1 cup warm water

Topping

6 tbsps passata

Olive oil

1 large eggplant,
cut into slices

Salt

2 beefsteak tomatoes, sliced

2 cloves garlic, sliced

Freshly ground black pepper

Fresh basil leaves

1. Sift the flour and salt into a warm mixing bowl and stir in the yeast. Make a well in the center, and add the olive oil and enough water to mix to a soft dough (you may not need all the water).

2. Turn out onto a floured surface and knead for a few minutes, until the dough is soft but not sticky. Shape into a round ball and roll out to form a circle 10 inches in diameter.

3. Place the dough on a lightly oiled cookie sheet and prick all over with a fork. Spread the base with the passata. Allow to stand in a warm place while preparing the topping.

4. Heat about 4 tbsps olive oil in a large skillet and fry the eggplant slices on both sides until beginning to brown. You may need to do this in batches; add extra olive oil as required.

5. Arrange alternate slices of eggplant and tomato on top of the pizza. Sprinkle with garlic and season well. Tear the basil into pieces and scatter on top.

6. Drizzle with olive oil and bake in a preheated 400°F oven for 25 to 30 minutes, or until the base is cooked and golden.

TIME Preparation takes about 30 minutes and cooking takes about 40 minutes.

Serves 4–6

Smoked Tofu Kedgeree with Almonds

TOFU IS EXTREMELY POPULAR IN THE FAR EAST, WHERE IT IS REGARDED AS HAVING ALMOST MAGICAL QUALITIES. HERE, IT IS VALUED FOR BEING LOW IN FAT AND HIGH IN PROTEIN.

Ingredients

1 cup long-grain brown rice

1 tsp salt

3 eggs

2 tbsps butter

1 tbsp grapeseed or safflower oil

1 cup smoked tofu, drained, pressed dry, and cut into ¾-inch cubes

2 tbsps flaked almonds

5 tbsps chopped fresh parsley or chives

Salt and freshly ground black pepper

1. Rinse the rice and place it in a pan with the salt and enough water to cover by the depth of your thumb. Bring to a boil, cover tightly, and simmer over a very low heat for 30 to 40 minutes, until all the liquid is absorbed.

2. Meanwhile, put the eggs in a pan, cover with water, and bring to a boil. Boil for 5 minutes exactly, then remove from the heat and drain. Remove the shells and coarsely chop the white and yolk.

3. Tip the rice into a warmed serving bowl, breaking up any lumps with a fork. Stir in the eggs and butter, and keep warm.

4. Heat the oil in a small pan and gently fry the tofu for a minute or two, until heated through. Add it to the rice and eggs. Fry the almonds until golden brown and add them to the rice.

5. Stir in the parsley and a little more butter, if necessary. Season with salt and pepper, and serve.

TIME Preparation takes 20 minutes and cooking takes 40 minutes.

Parsley *In the past, parsley was used more as a medicinal herb than a culinary one. It is widely used today, however, as a flavoring and garnish for a wide range of dishes. The two most common types of parsley are the curly-leaved variety, which is often used to make sauces, and common parsley, whose flat leaves can be a little more subtle in flavor.*

Serves 4

Herbed Lentil Stew

THIS TYPICAL MIDDLE EASTERN STEW IS A HEARTY
AND HEALTHFUL MIX OF LENTILS, SPINACH, AND
POTATOES, FLAVORED WITH LEMON AND GARLIC.

Ingredients

2 cups red lentils

3 cups water

2 tbsps vegetable oil

1 large onion, sliced

2 garlic cloves, minced

2 tbsps chopped fresh cilantro

1 pound spinach, trimmed
and chopped.

2 potatoes, peeled

Juice of 1 lemon

½ tsp salt

¼ tsp cayenne pepper

TIME Preparation takes
15 minutes and cooking takes
about 1½ hours.

1. Wash the lentils and pick them over to
remove any small stones or other
impurities. Put the lentils in a pan and
add water. Bring to a boil over high
heat, then reduce the heat, cover the
pan, and cook for 20 minutes.

2. Heat the oil in a 2-quart heatproof
casserole or Dutch oven. Add the onion
and cook over medium heat until the
onion is transparent—about 5 minutes.

3. Add the garlic and cilantro, and cook
5 minutes more. Add the spinach and
cook for another 5 minutes, stirring
constantly.

4. Add the potatoes and lentils with their
cooking liquid to the pan. Bring to a
boil over a high heat, then reduce the
heat, cover the pan, and simmer for
1 hour, or until thick. Add the lemon
juice, salt, and black pepper just before
serving.

Serves 4

Moors and Christians

ORIGINALLY FROM CUBA, THE BLACK BEANS AND
WHITE RICE IN THIS RECIPE REPRESENT THE OPPOSING
FORCES WHEN THE SARACENS INVADED SPAIN.

Ingredients

1 cup black beans, soaked
overnight and cooked until soft

2 tbsps vegetable oil

1 onion, chopped

4 cloves garlic, minced

1 green bell pepper, cored and
finely chopped

2 large tomatoes, peeled and
finely chopped

1¼ cups long-grain rice

Salt and freshly ground
black pepper

Little bean cooking water
if required

1. Drain the cooked beans and mash
   3 tbsps to a paste with a fork, adding a
   little bean cooking water, if necessary.

2. Heat the oil in a large pan and
   fry the onion, garlic, and bell pepper
   until soft.

3. Add the tomatoes and cook for
   2 minutes. Add the bean paste and stir.

4. Add the cooked beans and rice, and
   enough water to cover. Bring to a boil,
   cover, and simmer for 20 to 25
   minutes, until the rice is just cooked.
   Serve hot.

TIME Preparation takes 15 minutes.
Cooking takes 1 to 1½ hours for the
beans and 25 minutes for the finished dish.

VARIATION A small can of tomatoes
may be used in place of fresh ones.

Left: Moors and Christians

Serves 4

Mushroom and Herb Risotto

FRESH CHOPPED MIXED HERBS ADD A VIBRANT FLAVOR TO THIS APPETIZING RISOTTO,
WHICH IS IDEAL SERVED WITH FRESH CRUSTY BREAD AND A GREEN SALAD.

Ingredients

1 red onion, chopped

3 leeks, washed and thinly sliced

2 cloves garlic, minced

1 red bell pepper, cored and diced

4 celery sticks, chopped

1 cup long-grain brown rice

1¼ cups sliced button mushrooms

1¼ cups brown-cap
mushrooms, sliced

2½ cups vegetable broth

1¼ cups dry white wine

Salt and freshly ground
black pepper

7-ounce can corn, drained

½ cup frozen peas

3-4 tbsps chopped fresh
mixed herbs

4 tbsps fresh Parmesan cheese
shavings

Fresh herb sprigs to garnish

1. Place the onion, leek, garlic, bell pepper, celery, rice, mushrooms, broth, wine, and seasoning in a large pan, and stir to mix.

2. Bring to a boil and simmer, uncovered, for 25 to 30 minutes, stirring occasionally, until almost all the liquid has been absorbed.

3. Stir in the corn and peas and cook gently for about 10 minutes, stirring occasionally.

4. Stir in the chopped herbs and stir again to mix. Serve sprinkled with Parmesan cheese shavings and fresh herb sprigs.

TIME Preparation takes 15 minutes
and cooking takes 45 minutes.

Red Onions *This variety of onion is used
extensively in Asian and Mediterranean cooking and is
becoming much more popular elsewhere. As well as an
attractive color, the red onion has a sweet flavor that
makes it perfect for using raw or lightly cooked.*

Serves 6

Rice Pilaf with Dried Cranberries

WITH ITS FRUITY FLAVORS, THIS BRIGHTLY COLORED WILD AND BASMATI
RICE PILAF MAKES A BEAUTIFUL VEGETARIAN MAIN COURSE.

Ingredients

1 red onion, very finely chopped

1¼ cups vegetable broth

3 tender celery sticks, leaves
included, finely sliced

3 carrots, coarsely grated

1 green chili, seeded and finely
chopped

4 green onions, green parts
included, thinly sliced

⅓ cup dried cranberries

1 tbsp olive oil

2¼ cups cooked wild rice

1 cup cooked brown basmati rice

Finely grated rind
of 1 small orange

Juice of 3 small oranges
(about ½ cup)

1 tsp salt

¼ tsp freshly ground
black pepper

TIME Preparation takes
25 minutes, plus rice cooking
time. Cooking takes 10 minutes.

1. Place the onion and 6 tablespoons of broth in a large nonstick skillet. Cook for 3 to 4 minutes, until translucent.

2. Add the celery, carrots, chilies, green onions, and cranberries. Cook over medium heat for 2 minutes, until the vegetables are just tender but still crisp and brightly colored. Remove from the pan and set aside.

3. Add the oil to the pan over high heat. Stir in the rice and toss for 2 minutes to heat through. Lower the heat and stir in the grated orange rind, juice, remaining broth, and salt and pepper. Simmer for 1 minute.

4. Return the vegetables to the pan and toss with the rice to heat through before serving.

5. Serve the pilaf with Indian bread or pita pockets and a bowl of plain yogurt.

Serves 4

Cabbage Parcels

STUFFED CABBAGE LEAVES ARE POPULAR IN MANY COUNTRIES, ESPECIALLY IN
EASTERN EUROPE. A TASTY TOMATO SAUCE IS ONE OF THE BEST ACCOMPANIMENTS.

Ingredients

4 ounces soup pasta

8-12 large cabbage leaves, washed

1 hard-cooked egg, finely chopped

½ cup walnuts, chopped

1 tbsp chopped fresh chives

2 tbsps chopped fresh parsley

1 tsp chopped fresh marjoram

Salt and freshly ground
black pepper

1¼ cups vegetable broth

1 tbsp walnut oil

1 onion, finely chopped

1 green bell pepper,
cored and chopped

14-ounce can chopped tomatoes

1 cup button mushrooms,
chopped

2 tbsps tomato paste

1 bay leaf

Pinch of sugar

1. Cook the pasta in plenty of lightly salted, boiling water for 8 minutes, or as directed on the package.

2. Remove the thick stems from the base of the cabbage leaves and then blanch the leaves in boiling water for 3 minutes. Drain and refresh in cold water.

3. When the pasta is cooked, drain well and mix with the egg, walnuts, herbs, and seasoning to taste.

4. Divide the pasta mixture between the cabbage leaves, fold up to enclose the filling completely, and secure with toothpicks.

5. Place in a shallow, ovenproof dish and add the broth. Cover and bake in a preheated 350°F oven for 40 minutes.

6. Heat the oil in a skillet, add the onion and bell pepper, and fry for about 5 minutes, until soft. Stir in the remaining ingredients, season, and cook gently for 10 minutes.

7. Remove the cabbage parcels from the dish, remove the toothpicks and serve with the sauce poured over.

TIME Preparation takes 30 minutes and cooking takes about 1 hour.

Serves 4

Vegetable Stir-fry with Tofu

THE INCLUSION OF TOFU IN THIS RECIPE MAKES IT
AN EXCELLENT PROTEIN MEAL.

Ingredients

4 tbsps vegetable oil

1 ounce blanched almonds

1 clove garlic, minced

4 ounces baby corn, cut in half

1 red bell pepper, cored
and sliced

4 ounces snow peas, trimmed

2 ounces water chestnuts, sliced

2 heads of broccoli, split
into flowerets

4 tbsps soy sauce

1 tsp sesame oil

1 tsp sherry

⅔ cup vegetable broth

2 tsps cornstarch

2 cups bean sprouts

4 green onions, cut into
thin diagonal slices

8 ounces tofu, cut into cubes

Salt and freshly ground
black pepper

1. Heat the oil in a wok or skillet and fry the almonds until browned. Remove with a draining spoon and set aside.

2. Add the garlic and baby corn to the pan, and stir-fry for 1 minute. Stir in the bell pepper, snow peas, water chestnuts, and broccoli flowerets, and stir-fry for 4 minutes.

3. Mix the soy sauce, sesame oil, sherry, broth, and cornstarch together in a small dish and stir until blended. Add to the pan and stir until sauce thickens.

4. Add the bean sprouts, browned almonds, green onions, and tofu, and cook for 3 minutes. Season to taste and serve at once.

TIME Preparation takes about 20 minutes
and cooking takes 10 to 12 minutes.

Serves 4

Asian Ratatouille with Gingered Rice

THIS MEDITERRANEAN-STYLE VEGETABLE STEW IS GIVEN AN ORIENTAL TWIST
WITH SOME WARMING GINGER, SOY SAUCE, AND SESAME SEEDS.

Ingredients

5 tbsps light olive oil

1 small red onion, cut into
¾-inch squares

2 garlic cloves, minced

1-inch piece fresh ginger root,
minced

3 cups plum tomatoes, peeled,
seeded, and chopped

2 tbsps tamari (Japanese soy
sauce) or shoyu

1½ tbsps rice wine

1 tsp sugar

Salt and freshly ground
black pepper

1 fresh green chili, seeded and
chopped

2 tsps coriander seeds, crushed

1 small eggplant, cut into
¾-inch chunks

⅔ cup sliced shittake mushrooms

2 small zucchini, sliced diagonally

1 red bell pepper, cored and
cut into chunks

2 tsps sesame seeds, toasted

Rice

3 tbsps groundnut oil

1-2 tsps hot chili oil

2 garlic cloves, minced

1-inch piece fresh ginger root,
minced

1½ cups medium-grain white rice

1½ cups light vegetable broth

1¼ cups water

Salt

2 tbsps fresh lime or lemon juice

4 green onions, finely chopped

2 tbsps minced fresh
cilantro leaves

TIME Preparation takes about
35 minutes and cooking takes
45 minutes.

1. Heat 1 tbsp of the olive oil in a saucepan. Add the onion and gently fry for 5 minutes, until just soft. Add the garlic and ginger, and fry for 1 minute. Stir in the tomatoes, tamari, rice wine, and sugar. Season with salt and pepper. Simmer over a very low heat for 15 to 20 minutes, stirring occasionally, until reduced and thickened.

2. Meanwhile, prepare the rice. Heat the oils in a skillet with a lid. Add the garlic and ginger root, and fry for one minute. Add the rice and cook for 3 to 4 minutes, stirring, until all the grains are coated with oil. Pour in the broth, water, and a little salt. Bring to a boil, then cover tightly and simmer over very low heat for 15 to 20 minutes, until all the liquid has been absorbed. Remove from the heat and stir in the juice. Leave to stand, covered, for 10 minutes.

3. Meanwhile, heat the remaining olive oil in a large skillet until very hot. Add the chili pepper and coriander seeds, and sizzle for 30 seconds. Add the eggplant and shittake mushrooms, and stir-fry over medium heat for 5 minutes. Stir in the remaining vegetables and fry for 3 more minutes.

4. When the vegetables are just soft, pour in the tomato sauce, cover, and simmer for 10 minutes. Check the seasoning and stir in the sesame seeds.

5. Stir the green onions and cilantro into the rice, and serve with the vegetables.

Serves 4 – 6

Lentil Moussaka

TRY A TASTE OF THE GREEK ISLANDS WITH
THIS VARIATION ON A CLASSIC DISH.

Ingredients

1¾ cups green lentils

1 large eggplant, sliced

4-5 tbsps vegetable oil

1 large onion, chopped

1 clove garlic, minced

1 large carrot, diced

4 celery sticks, finely chopped

1-2 tsps mixed herbs

14-ounce can tomatoes

2 tsps Japanese soy sauce

Freshly ground black pepper

2 potatoes, cooked and sliced

2 large tomatoes, sliced

Sauce

4 tbsps margarine

4 tbsps brown rice flour

Scant 2 cups milk

1 large egg, separated

½ cup grated Cheddar cheese

1 tsp nutmeg

1. Cook the lentils in plenty of water until soft. Drain and reserve the liquid.

2. Fry the eggplant in the oil, drain well, and set aside. Cook the onion, garlic, carrot and celery in a little of the lentil stock, simmering with the lid on until just tender.

3. Add the lentils, mixed herbs, and canned tomatoes. Simmer gently for 3 to 4 minutes. Season with the soy sauce and pepper.

4. Place a layer of the lentil mixture in a large casserole dish and cover with half of the eggplant slices. Cover the eggplant slices with half of the potato slices and all the tomato. Repeat with the remaining lentils, eggplant, and potatoes.

5. To make the sauce, gently melt the margarine in a saucepan, remove from the heat, and stir in the flour.

6. Add the milk gradually, blending well, so that the sauce is smooth and reasonably lump free. Return to the heat and stir continually until the sauce thickens. Remove the pan from the heat and cool slightly. Add the egg yolk, stir in the cheese, and add the nutmeg.

7. Beat the egg white until it is stiff, then carefully fold into the sauce.

8. Pour the sauce over the moussaka, covering the dish completely. Bake in a preheated 350°F oven for about 40 minutes, until the top is golden brown and puffy.

TIME Preparation takes 45 minutes and cooking takes 1 hour 10 minutes.

Serves 4

Vegetarian Garbure

THIS IS A VEGETARIAN VARIATION OF A CLASSIC FRENCH COUNTRY STEW. SERVED
WITH FRESH WHOLE-WHEAT BREAD, IT MAKES A WARMING LUNCH OR SUPPER DISH.

Ingredients

1⅓ cups navy beans, soaked
overnight

1 large potato, scrubbed and diced

4 carrots, sliced

2 leeks, washed and chopped

2 tbsps vegetable oil

1 tsp dried marjoram

1 tsp dried thyme

½ tsp paprika pepper

3¾ cups vegetable broth

Salt and freshly ground
black pepper

1 small cabbage, finely shredded

Whole-wheat bread, to serve

1. Drain the beans and place them in a
pan with enough fresh water to cover
them by 1 inch. Bring to a boil, boil
rapidly for 10 minutes, then lower the
heat and simmer gently for 1 hour, or
until the beans are soft. Drain and set
aside until required.

2. Fry the potato, carrots, and leeks in the
oil for 5 minutes. Add the herbs and
paprika, and cook for 1 minute. Stir in
the beans and broth, and simmer gently
for 20 minutes.

3. Stir the bean mixture and season to
taste. Scatter the shredded cabbage over
the beans, cover and continue cooking
for 15 to 20 minutes, until the cabbage
is cooked. Check the seasoning and
serve with the bread.

TIME Preparation takes 20 minutes, plus
overnight soaking. Cooking takes about
1¾ hours.

SERVING IDEA Place thick slices of
bread in the bottom of some soup bowls
and then ladle the Garbure over the
bread—delicious!

Paprika   *This brightly colored spice is made
from capsicums or red bell peppers. There are two types
of paprika, hot and sweet, although the type is often not stated
on the label. Hot paprika is obtained by including the inner core and
seeds of the pepper, while sweet paprika is made by adding sugar.*

Serves 4

Parmesan Soufflé Omelet

OMELETS ARE A WONDERFUL CONVENIENCE FOOD FOR VEGETARIANS. THIS PUFFY
OMELET IS FLAVORED WITH FRESH, CHOPPED CHIVES AND PARMESAN CHEESE.

Ingredients

8 eggs, separated

Scant ½ cup milk

¾ cup grated Parmesan cheese

2 tbsps chopped chives

Salt and freshly ground
black pepper

1 tbsp oil

2 tbsps butter

1. Mix the egg yolks into the milk with the Parmesan, chives, salt, and pepper.

2. Whip the egg whites until very stiff, and then gently incorporate the yolk mixture into the whites.

3. Heat the oil and the butter in a large frying pan and cook both sides of the omelet until golden brown. Serve immediately.

COOK'S TIP Turning a large omelet like this one can be quite a difficult task. As an alternative, use a small frying pan and cook individual omelets for your guests, keeping the first ones warm in an open oven.

TIME Preparation takes about 15 minutes and cooking takes 10 to 15 minutes.

Butter *The importance of butter to good cooking cannot be overstressed–without it haute cuisine just wouldn't exist. Butter adds a rich creaminess and distinct flavor to dishes that cannot be matched by margarine, despite what the marketing people may have you believe. The cholesterol content of butter cannot be denied, but, like with all rich foods, moderation is the key.*

Serves 4

Fettuccine with Blue Cheese Sauce

MANY PASTA DISHES CAN BE RATHER FATTENING. THIS ONE, HOWEVER, USES ONLY
A SMALL AMOUNT OF STRONG CHEESE TO ENHANCE THE PASTA AND SPINACH.

Ingredients

1 pound fettuccine

2 tbsps soft margarine

1 clove garlic, minced

4 shallots, finely chopped

2 tbsps all-purpose flour

2 cups low-fat milk

3 cups cooked, drained spinach

⅓ cup blue cheese, crumbled

Salt and freshly ground
black pepper

Finely chopped fresh parsley,
to garnish

TIME Preparation takes
15 minutes and cooking takes
15 minutes.

VARIATION Use 1 small
standard or red onion, or 1 bunch
of green onions in place of the
shallots.

1. Cook the pasta in a large pan of lightly
salted, boiling water for 10 to 12
minutes, until just cooked or al dente.

2. Meanwhile, make the spinach and blue
cheese sauce. Melt the margarine in a
saucepan, add the garlic and shallots,
and cook gently for 5 minutes, stirring.

3. Add the flour and cook for 1 minute,
stirring. Remove the pan from the heat
and gradually stir in the milk. Heat
gently, stirring continuously, until the
sauce comes to a boil and thickens.
Reduce the heat and simmer gently for
3 minutes, stirring.

4. Press any excess water out of the
spinach using the back of a wooden
spoon, then chop the spinach. Add the
spinach, cheese, and seasoning to the
sauce and mix well. Reheat gently,
stirring continuously, until the cheese
has melted and the sauce is piping hot.

5. Drain the cooked pasta thoroughly,
then toss it with the sauce and serve
immediately, garnished with some
minced parsley. Alternatively, serve the
pasta with the sauce spooned over it.
Serve this dish with crusty bread rolls
and a mixed leaf salad.

Serves 4

Spicy Oriental Noodles

THIS VERSATILE CHINESE VEGETABLE DISH MAKES
AN EXCELLENT VEGETARIAN MAIN COURSE.

Ingredients

8 ounces Chinese noodles
(medium thickness)

5 tbsps oil

4 carrots, cut into thinly sliced
rounds

8 ounces broccoli, cut into flowerets

4 green onions, diagonally sliced

12 Chinese mushrooms,
soaked 30 minutes

1 clove garlic, peeled

1-2 tsps chili sauce, mild or hot

4 tbsps soy sauce

4 tbsps rice wine or dry sherry

2 tsps cornstarch

1. Cook the noodles in boiling, salted water for about 4 to 5 minutes. Drain well, rinse under hot water to remove starch, and drain again. Toss with about 1 tbsp of the oil to prevent sticking.

2. Place the carrots, broccoli, and green onions in boiling water for about 2 minutes to blanch. Drain and rinse under cold water to stop them cooking, and leave to drain dry. Remove and discard the mushroom stems and slice the caps thinly. Set aside with the other vegetables.

3. Heat a wok and add the remaining oil with the garlic clove. Leave the garlic in the pan while the oil heats and them remove it. Add the carrots and broccoli, and stir-fry about 1 minute. Add mushrooms and onions, and continue to stir-fry, tossing the vegetables in the pan continuously.

4. Combine the chili sauce, soy sauce, wine, and cornstarch, mixing well. Pour over the vegetables and cook until the sauce clears. Add the noodles, toss together well to heat them through, and serve immediately.

Time Preparation takes about 25 minutes
and cooking takes 7 to 8 minutes.

Noodles *A mainstay of the Chinese diet, noodles are available in various forms, with the quick-cooking egg-thread noodles and rice noodles being particularly popular. Many types of noodle are sold in compressed blocks, having been pre-steamed before packing.*

Serves 4

Vegetable Chop Suey

WITH VEGETABLES, SIMPLE TREATMENTS ARE USUALLY THE BEST. HERE, STIR-FRIED
VEGETABLES ARE SIMMERED IN A WOK WITH BROTH AND SOY SAUCE.

Ingredients

2 tbsps vegetable oil

1 green bell pepper, cored and
thinly sliced

1 red bell pepper, cored and
thinly sliced

2 cloves garlic, finely chopped

1 onion, thinly sliced

1 carrot, thinly sliced

½ cucumber, thinly sliced

1 zucchini, central core
discarded and flesh thinly sliced

2 tsps sugar

2 tbsps soy sauce

½ cup vegetable broth

Salt and freshly ground
black pepper

1. Heat the oil in a wok and stir-fry the
bell peppers and garlic for 30 seconds.
Add the onion and the carrot and stir-
fry for another 30 seconds.

2. Add the cucumber and the zucchini,
and cook for 1 minute, stirring and
shaking the wok continuously.

3. Stir in the sugar, soy sauce, vegetable
broth, salt, and pepper, mixing together
well. Simmer until all the ingredients
are heated through. Serve piping hot.

COOK'S TIP If you follow the order given
above for cooking the vegetables, they will
be cooked but still slightly crisp.

TIME Preparation takes about
15 minutes and cooking takes
5 minutes.

Cinnamon *This useful spice is obtained from the bark
of the cinnamon tree (cinnamon sticks are rolled pieces of bark),
which grows wild in Sri Lanka and southern India. It has
been valued for its subtle flavor for centuries and was at
one point among the most valuable commodities
traded between Sri Lanka and Europe.*

Serves 4

Saagwalla Daal

SPINACH AND DAAL COMPLEMENT EACH OTHER WELL. THE DISH IS EASY TO MAKE AND FULL OF ESSENTIAL NUTRIENTS. IF MOONG DAAL IS UNAVAILABLE, USE YELLOW SPLIT PEAS.

Ingredients

¼ cup skinless split moong daal or yellow split peas

2 heaping tbsps ghee or unsalted butter

1 large onion, finely sliced

1 fresh green chili, sliced lengthwise

2 cinnamon sticks, each 2 inches long, broken up into 2-3 pieces

½ tsp ground turmeric

½ tsp garam masala

¼ tsp chili powder

1 tsp salt or to taste

1 tsp ground cumin

2 ripe tomatoes, peeled and chopped

2½ cups warm water

2 tbsps cooking oil

½ tsp mustard seeds

2-3 cloves garlic, finely chopped

1-2 dried red chilies, coarsely chopped

5 ounces leaf spinach, defrosted and finely chopped, or 10 ounces fresh spinach, stalks removed and finely chopped

1. Wash the daal, then soak it for 1½ to 2 hours and drain well.

2. Melt the ghee or butter in a nonstick or cast iron skillet, add the onions, chili, and cinnamon, and fry for 6 to 8 minutes, until the onions are lightly browned.

3. Add the turmeric and garam masala, stir and mix well. Add the daal, chili powder, and salt. Stir and fry for 8 to 10 minutes over low heat.

4. Add the cumin and tomato, stir and cook for 3 to 4 minutes.

5. Add the water, bring to a boil, cover and simmer for 30 to 35 minutes, stirring occasionally.

6. Meanwhile, heat the oil over medium heat and fry the mustard seeds until they pop. Add the garlic and allow it to turn slightly brown.

7. Add the dried chilies and spinach, and stir and mix thoroughly. Cover the pan and simmer for 5 minutes.

8. Add the spinach to the daal, cover and cook over low heat for 10 minutes, stirring occasionally. Remove the pan from heat and serve.

TIME Preparation takes 10 to 15 minutes, plus time needed to soak the daal. Cooking takes 1 hour 10 minutes.

Vegetable Enchiladas

TEX-MEX COOKING INCLUDES SOME WONDERFUL SAUCES.
HERE, A REFRESHING SALSA COMPLEMENTS A VEGETABLE FILLING.

Ingredients

4 tortillas

Sour cream to serve

Green chili salsa

1 tbsp oil

*3 tomatillos, husks removed
and sliced*

1 clove garlic

1 ounce ground coriander

2 green chilies

Juice of 1 lime

½ cup sour cream

Pinch of salt and sugar

Filling

2 tbsps vegetable oil

1 small onion, finely chopped

*1 green bell pepper,
seeded and diced*

2 zucchini, diced

½ tsp oregano

½ tsp ground cumin

4 ounces corn, fresh or frozen

Salt and freshly ground black pepper

1½ cups grated mild cheese

1. Heat the oil for the salsa in a small skillet and sauté the tomatillos for about 3 minutes to soften. Place in a food processor or blender with the garlic, coriander, chilies, and lime juice. Purée until smooth. Fold in the ½ cup sour cream, add seasoning, and chill.

2. Wrap the tortillas in foil and re-heat in a moderate oven for about 10 minutes.

3. For the filling, heat the oil, add the onion, and cook to soften. Add the remaining vegetables, except the corn. Add the oregano and cumin, and cook about 3 minutes, or until the onions are soft. Add the corn and heat through. Add seasoning to taste and stir in the grated cheese.

4. Fill the tortillas with the mixture and place in a baking dish. Cook, covered, in a preheated 350°F oven for about 10 to 15 minutes, until the cheese has melted and the filling is beginning to bubble.

5. Remove the vegetable enchiladas from the oven and serve topped with sour cream and green chili salsa.

TIME Preparation takes about 20 minutes
and cooking takes about 30 minutes.

Eggs *The number of recipes based on eggs that can be found around the world is testament to the vital role they have played in our diet for centuries. Many of the recipes that we believe to be Western, such as omelets, can actually be found in various guises from South America to Asia.*

Serves 6

Cheese Soufflé

THIS PUFFY, GOLDEN SOUFFLÉ WILL DELIGHT YOUR GUESTS, BUT RUSH
IT TO THE TABLE IMMEDIATELY ON REMOVAL FROM THE OVEN!

1. Grease a soufflé dish with butter and sprinkle with 3 tbsps of the grated cheese.

2. Melt the butter in a heavy saucepan, mix in the flour, cook for about 1 minute, pour in all the milk, and beat continuously until the mixture thickens. Reduce the heat and cook for 2 minutes.

3. Add the salt, pepper, nutmeg, and egg yolks one by one, beating well with a wooden spoon. Leave to cool for about 5 minutes.

4. Stir the remaining cheese into the white sauce. Whisk the 5 egg whites until firm, then fold them gently into the cheese mixture with a metal spoon.

5. Pour the mixture into the prepared soufflé dish and cook in a preheated 375°F oven for 40 to 45 minutes. The soufflé should be well risen and golden on top. Serve immediately.

Ingredients

Butter for greasing

1½ cups grated cheese

2 tbsps butter

1 tbsp all-purpose flour

1¼ cups milk

Salt and freshly ground black pepper

Pinch of nutmeg

4 eggs, separated

1 extra egg white

SERVING IDEAS At step 5, the mixture could be poured into 6 individual buttered and "cheesed" custard cups. Cooking time will be reduced to 20 to 25 minutes.

TIME Preparation takes about 20 minutes, and cooking takes 40 to 45 minutes.

Serves 6

Black Bean and Squash Casserole

EAST MEETS WEST IN THIS UNUSUAL DISH, WHICH MIXES AROMATIC SPICES WITH
FAMILIAR ROOT VEGETABLES.

Ingredients

2 cups cooked black
turtle beans

1 tsp cumin seeds

2 tsps coriander seeds

1 tbsp sesame seeds

2 tsps dried oregano

2 tbsps olive oil

1 onion, chopped

2 garlic cloves, minced

1-2 fresh red chilies,
seeded and chopped

1 butternut squash or small
pumpkin, weighing about
1¼ pounds, peeled and
cut into chunks

1 yellow yam or sweet potato,
peeled and cut into chunks

2 large carrots, thickly sliced

2 potatoes, peeled and
cut into chunks

1 celery root, weighing
about 1 pound, peeled and
cut into chunks

3 ounces frozen corn

14-ounce can chopped tomatoes

1½ cups vegetable broth

Salt and freshly ground
black pepper

4 tbsps chopped fresh
cilantro leaves

2 tbsps lime juice

1. Heat the seeds in a small skillet for 1 to 2 minutes. Add the oregano and heat for a few more seconds. Remove and crush.

2. Heat the oil in a casserole, add the onion, and fry until translucent. Add the garlic and chilies, and fry for 2 to 3 minutes.

3. Add the seeds and the remaining ingredients, except the cilantro leaves and lime juice. Bring to a boil, cover, and simmer for 45 minutes. Add the cilantro and lime juice just before serving.

TIME Preparation takes 25 minutes. Cooking takes 1 hour 20 minutes.

Squash *The large variety of squashes we see in our supermarkets is largely the result of easy cross-pollination. Squashes, however, no matter how colorful or exotic in shape, are almost always bland in flavor and benefit from robust treatment. If you grow your own squash, try frying the partially opened flower buds in olive oil for an unusual and tasty dish.*

Serves 4

Red Bean Creole

CREOLE COOKING IS A BLEND OF AFRICAN, CARIBBEAN, AND INDIAN CUISINE THAT REFLECTS PAST TRADING LINKS. THE EMPHASIS IS ON SPICING UP LOCAL INGREDIENTS.

Ingredients

Scant cup long-grain brown or white rice

2 tbsps butter or margarine

1 green bell pepper, cored and sliced

Generous 1¼ cups sliced mushrooms

Pinch of cayenne pepper

Pinch of ground nutmeg

2 cups red kidney beans, cooked

⅓ cup vegetable broth

4 firm tomatoes, peeled, seeded, and cut into strips

4 green onions, trimmed and chopped

Salt and freshly ground black pepper

Chopped fresh parsley to garnish

1. Cook the rice in plenty of boiling water as directed on the package. Drain and rinse with boiling water.

2. Melt the butter in a large saucepan, add the bell pepper and mushrooms, and cook for about 5 minutes, until just beginning to soften.

3. Add the rice, cayenne pepper, nutmeg, beans, and broth. Cook gently for 10 minutes, stir in the remaining ingredients and cook for another 5 minutes to heat all the ingredients thoroughly. Serve garnished with chopped parsley.

SERVING IDEA Serve with a small side salad or a bowl of ratatouille—each is as good as the other.

TIME Preparation takes 20 minutes and cooking takes about 40 minutes.

Nutmeg *Nutmeg is obtained from the seed of a tree cultivated in tropical regions. The fruits are harvested when ripe, the outer shell is removed and the seeds allowed to dry. Nutmeg has a strong aroma and is used only in small quantities.*

The World Vegetarian Cookbook 91

Serves 4

Gado Gado

THIS DELICIOUS INDONESIAN DISH HAS BECOME A FIRM VEGETARIAN FAVORITE.
IT IS HEALTHY, EASY TO PREPARE, AND A REAL TASTE BUD TICKLER.

Ingredients

2 tbsps peanut oil

2 carrots, cut into thin strips

2 potatoes, cut into thin strips

8 ounces green beans, trimmed

8 ounces Chinese cabbage, shredded

8 ounces bean sprouts

Half a cucumber, cut into batons

Peanut sauce

4 tbsps peanut oil

¾ cup raw shelled peanuts

4 red chilies, seeded and
finely chopped

4 shallots, finely chopped

2 cloves garlic, minced

2 tsps brown sugar

Juice of half a lemon

Scant 1 cup coconut milk

⅔ cup water

Salt

Garnish

Sliced hard-cooked eggs

Sliced cucumbers

1. Heat a wok and add 2 tbsps peanut oil. When hot, toss in carrot and potato. Stir-fry for 2 minutes and add green beans and cabbage. Cook for 3 minutes.

2. Add the bean sprouts and cucumber, and stir-fry for 2 minutes. Remove the vegetables, place in a serving dish and chill.

3. Heat the wok, add the peanut oil, and fry the peanuts for 2 to 3 minutes. Remove and drain on paper towels. Blend or pound the chilies, shallots, and garlic to a smooth paste. Grind or blend the peanuts to a powder.

4. Heat the peanut oil, add the chili paste, and fry for 2 minutes. Add the water and bring to a boil. Add the peanuts, brown sugar, lemon juice, and salt to taste. Heat, stirring until sauce is thick—about 10 minutes—and add coconut milk.

5. Garnish the vegetables with slices of hard-cooked egg and cucumber, and serve with the peanut sauce.

TIME Preparation takes 20 minutes
and cooking takes 30 minutes.

Serves 4

Cauliflower Masala

CAULIFLOWER IS PARTICULARLY DELICIOUS CURRIED, WHEN IT SEEMS TO SOAK UP
ALL THE FLAVORS WHILE RETAINING ITS CHARACTERISTIC TEXTURE.

Ingredients

4 tbsps vegetable oil

1 tsp cumin seeds

1 large onion, chopped

½ tsp ground turmeric

1 tsp ground coriander

1 tsp ground cumin

¼-½ tsp chili powder

2 ripe tomatoes, peeled
and chopped

2 potatoes, peeled and cut into
thick batons

¾ cup warm water

1 cauliflower, cut into flowerets

½ cup shelled peas, fresh or
frozen (cook fresh peas until
they are tender before using)

1-2 fresh green chilies, seeded
and slit lengthwise into halves

1 tsp salt or to taste

½ tsp garam masala

1 tbsp chopped fresh cilantro
leaves

1. Heat the oil over medium heat and add the cumin seeds. As soon as they start popping, add the onion and fry for about 5 minutes until soft.

2. Turn heat down to low and add the turmeric, coriander, cumin, and chili powder. Stir and fry for 2 to 3 minutes and add the chopped tomatoes. Fry for another 2 to 3 minutes, stirring continuously.

3. Add the potatoes and the water. Bring to a boil, cover the pan, and simmer until the potatoes are half cooked.

4. Add the cauliflower, cover the pan again and simmer for about 10 minutes until the potatoes are tender.

5. Stir in the peas, chilies, salt, and garam masala. Cover and cook for 5 minutes. Remove from heat and stir in the chopped cilantro.

TIME Preparation takes about 25 minutes and cooking takes 30 to 35 minutes.

VARIATION Cook in 3 tbsps ghee or unsalted butter instead of oil for a richer flavor.

Serves 4–6

Egg and Potato Dum

HARD-COOKED, CURRIED EGGS ARE VERY POPULAR IN NORTHEAST INDIA,
WHERE THIS RECIPE ORIGINATES.

Ingredients

6 hard-cooked eggs

5 tbsps cooking oil

3 potatoes, peeled and quartered

⅛ tsp each of chili powder and
ground turmeric, mixed together

1 large onion, finely chopped

½-inch cube fresh ginger root,
peeled and grated

1 cinnamon stick, 2 inches long,
broken up into 2-3 pieces

2 black or green cardamoms,
split open at the top

4 whole cloves

1 fresh green chili, chopped

1 small can tomatoes

½ tsp ground turmeric

2 tsps ground coriander

1 tsp ground fennel

¼-½ tsp chili powder (optional)

1 tsp salt or to taste

1 cup warm water

1 tbsp chopped fresh cilantro leaves

1. Shell the eggs and make 4 slits lengthwise on each egg, leaving about ½-inch gap at either end.

2. Heat the oil over medium heat in a cast iron or nonstick skillet. Fry the potatoes until they are well browned on all sides, about 10 minutes. Remove with a slotted spoon and set aside.

3. Remove pan from the heat and stir in the turmeric and chili mixture. Place the pan on the heat and fry the whole eggs until they are well browned. Remove with a slotted spoon and set aside.

4. In the same oil, fry the onions, ginger, cinnamon, cardamom, cloves, and green chili for 6 to 7 minutes, until the onions are lightly browned.

5. Add half the tomatoes, stir and fry until the tomatoes break up. Add the turmeric, ground coriander, fennel, and chili powder. Stir and fry for 3 to 4 minutes. Add the remaining tomatoes and fry for 4 to 5 minutes, stirring frequently.

6. Add the potatoes, salt, and water, bring to a boil, cover the pan tightly, and simmer until the potatoes are tender, stirring occasionally.

7. Now add the eggs and simmer, uncovered, for 5 to 6 minutes, stirring once or twice. Stir in the cilantro leaves and serve.

TIME Preparation takes 15 minutes and cooking takes 35 to 40 minutes.

Serves 4 – 6

Eastern Mediterranean Casserole

BURSTING WITH COLOR AND FLAVOR, THIS COMFORTING CASSEROLE
MAKES AN EXCELLENT ENTRÉE FOR A FALL DINNER.

Ingredients

1 tsp cumin seeds

2 tsps coriander seeds

1 tbsp sesame seeds

2 tsps dried oregano

1 tsp vegetable oil

1 onion, chopped

3 garlic cloves, finely chopped

1 green chili, seeded and chopped

1½ cups strong vegetable broth

1 cup butternut squash or
pumpkin flesh, cut into chunks

1 small eggplant, cut into chunks

1 red bell pepper, cut into squares

6 ounces green beans, chopped

6 ounces small new potatoes,
unpeeled

14-ounce can peeled, chopped
tomatoes

Salt and freshly ground
black pepper

6 ounces shredded green
cabbage

1. Place the seeds in a small, heavy-based pan without any oil. Heat until the aroma rises. Add the oregano and dry-fry for a few more seconds. Remove from the heat, crush with a pestle and mortar, and set aside.

2. Heat the oil in a heavy-based, nonstick casserole. Gently fry the onion for a few minutes over medium-low heat until translucent. Add the garlic, chili, and 2 tbsp of the broth. Fry for 3 minutes, until soft. Stir in the seed mixture.

3. Add the squash, eggplant, bell pepper, beans, potatoes, and tomatoes. Bring to a boil, then cover and cook over medium-low heat for 10 minutes.

4. Pour in the remaining broth and season with salt and pepper. Bring to a boil, then cover and simmer for 20 minutes.

Add more broth if the mixture starts to look too dry.

5. Stir in the cabbage and cook for 2 to 3 minutes, until just wilted but still bright green. Serve immediately with cooked rice or cracked wheat.

TIME Preparation takes 25 minutes and cooking takes 45 minutes.

VARIATION Use 1 cup chopped mushrooms in place of the eggplant.

COOK'S TIP The toasted crushed seeds act as a thickener and also add a wonderfully earthy flavor to the dish.

Serves 4

Japanese Steamer

THE JAPANESE ARE RENOWNED FOR THEIR ELEGANT CUISINE, AND THIS SIMPLE
RECIPE IS NO EXCEPTION. SERVE FOR A DELICIOUS ORIENTAL-STYLE MEAL.

Ingredients

4 ounces buckwheat noodles

16 dried shittake mushrooms,
soaked overnight

1 cup button mushrooms

8 baby corn, halved lengthwise

1 small daikon (mooli) radish,
sliced

12 ounces tofu, drained

1 package dried sea spinach,
soaked for 1 hour

⅔ cup Japanese soy sauce

Small piece fresh ginger root,
peeled and grated

4 tbsps vegetable broth

1 tbsp sherry

1 tsp cornstarch

1 lemon, thinly sliced

1 small bunch fresh chives

1. Cook the noodles in plenty of lightly salted, boiling water for 10 minutes.

2. Remove the stems from the shittake mushrooms and discard. Steam the mushroom caps, button mushrooms, baby corn, and daikon for 5 to 10 minutes.

3. Cut the tofu into chunks and steam with the sea spinach for 2 minutes.

4. Make the sauce by heating the soy sauce, ginger root, and vegetable broth in a small pan until simmering. Blend the sherry and cornstarch together, add to the pan, and cook until thickened.

5. Drain the noodles and arrange along with the steamed vegetables on serving plates. Pour a little sauce over each and serve remaining sauce separately. Garnish with lemon slices and chives.

TIME Preparation takes about 30 minutes, plus overnight soaking. Cooking takes about 15 minutes.

Chives Chives are related to the onion and leek but impart a more subtle flavor. As well as the standard type of chive sold in supermarkets, you may also come across a dark green variety known as Chinese or garlic chives. This is a larger plant whose flattish leaves have a pronounced garlic flavor.

Serves 6

Eggplant Bake

IT MAY SEEM A CRIME TO ALL THOSE WHO LOVE THE FLAVOR OF EGGPLANTS, BUT
THIS WONDERFUL VEGETABLE WAS ONCE TREATED SIMPLY AS A DECORATIVE PLANT!

Ingredients

2 large or 3 medium eggplants

2½ tsps salt

⅔ cup malt vinegar

2½ tbsps vegetable oil

2 large onions, sliced into rings

2 green chilies, seeded and
finely chopped

2 cups peeled plum tomatoes,
chopped

¼ tsp chili powder

1¼ tsps minced garlic

¾ tsp ground turmeric

8 tomatoes, sliced

1⅓ cups plain yogurt

1¼ tsps freshly ground
black pepper

1 cup finely grated
cheddar cheese

1. Cut the eggplants into ¼-inch-thick
slices. Arrange the slices in a shallow
dish and sprinkle with 1½ tsps of the
salt. Pour over the malt vinegar, cover
the dish, and marinate for 30 minutes.
Drain the eggplant well, discarding the
marinade.

2. Heat the oil in a skillet and gently fry
the onion rings until golden brown. Add
the chilies, the remaining salt, chopped
tomatoes, chili powder, garlic, and
turmeric. Mix well and simmer for 5 to
7 minutes until thick and well blended.

3. Remove the sauce from the heat and
cool slightly. Blend to a smooth purée
using a food processor or blender.

4. Arrange half of the eggplant slices in
the base of a lightly greased shallow
ovenproof dish. Spoon half of the
tomato sauce over the eggplant slices.
Cover the tomato sauce with the
remaining eggplant, and then top this
with the remaining tomato sauce and
sliced tomatoes.

5. Mix together the yogurt, black pepper,
and cheese, and pour over the tomato
slices.

6. Bake in a preheated 375°F oven for
20 to 30 minutes, until the cheese
topping bubbles and turns golden
brown. Serve hot straight from the oven.

TIME Preparation takes about 30 minutes
and cooking takes 40 minutes.

PREPARATION Make sure that the
eggplants are well drained of excess
vinegar by pressing them into a colander
using the back of your hand. Do not rinse
them, however, as the vinegar gives a
tangy flavor to the dish.

Serves 4

Mushroom Stroganoff

WITH MUSHROOMS REPLACING THE MEAT, THIS DELICIOUS STROGANOFF IS FAR
TASTIER AND HEALTHIER THAN THE ORIGINAL RECIPE.

Ingredients

4 tbsps butter or margarine

2 onions, sliced

5 celery sticks, chopped

6 cups button mushrooms

½ tsp dried mixed herbs

½ tsp dried basil

1 heaping tbsp all-purpose flour

1¼ cups broth

Salt and freshly ground
black pepper

⅓ cup sour cream or
plain yogurt

Chopped fresh parsley,
to garnish

TIME Preparation takes 10 minutes and
cooking takes 20 minutes.

1. Melt the butter or margarine in a large
   pan, add the onions and celery,
   and sauté over a low heat until the
   onions are transparent.

2. Add the mushrooms and cook for 2 to
   3 minutes, until the juices run. Add the
   mixed herbs and basil, stir in the flour,
   and heat for 1 minute.

3. Add the broth and seasoning, and cook
   gently for 8 to 10 minutes. Remove from
   the heat, stir in the sour cream, and
   adjust the seasoning if necessary.

4. Heat very gently to serving temperature,
   but do not allow to boil. Garnish with the
   chopped parsley and serve at once.

C e l e r y *It is thought celery was first widely eaten
during the Middle Ages, when it began to be cultivated.
It is rich in mineral salts, vitamins, and iron and, although
often served raw, it is not easily digestible in this
form and is better cooked.*

SIDE DISHES

Side dishes are all too often overlooked by busy cooks yet they undoubtedly add an extra dimension to a meal, both in terms of nutrition and taste. Most people enjoy dipping into a variety of different dishes, and serving vegetables, breads, and rice with a contrasting main course produces a much more interesting meal. In this chapter you will find a cross-section of side dishes from around the world, including an Indian Carrot Pilau, Roasted Vegetables from the Mediterranean, and delicious Long Beans in Coconut Milk from Thailand. Also included are a number of delicious and easy-to-prepare breads from as far afield as Ireland, India, and Mexico.

Serves 6

Baked Pineapple Rice

THIS ATTRACTIVELY PRESENTED RICE DISH IS FROM
BANGKOK AND THE CENTRAL PLAINS OF THAILAND.

Ingredients

1 pineapple

2 tbsps oil

1 clove garlic, minced

4 shallots, chopped

1 pound cooked rice

⅔ cup thick coconut milk

2 tbsps raisins

2 tbsps toasted cashew nuts

Yellow curry paste

2 tbsps cumin seeds

2 tbsps coriander seeds

3 stems lemon grass, chopped

1 tbsp grated fresh ginger root

*6 red chilies, seeded
and chopped*

1 tsp salt

3 cloves garlic, minced

1 small shallot, finely chopped

1 tsp ground turmeric

1. Dry-fry the cumin and coriander seeds for 3 to 4 minutes, shaking the pan to prevent them burning. Remove from the heat and set aside. Place the lemon grass and ginger in a pestle and mortar, and pound together well. Add the chilies and salt and pound again. Add the chilies, shallot, ground spices, and turmeric, and pound all together well. Set aside.

2. Cut the pineapple in half lengthwise, keeping the leaves attached. Scoop out the flesh using a tablespoon and a paring knife to leave two shells with a thin border of flesh attached. Chop half the flesh to use later in the dish (the remainder is not needed for this recipe).

3. Heat the oil in a wok and fry the garlic and shallots until softened. Stir in 1 tbsp of curry paste and fry for 1 minute. Add the rice and toss together with the shallot mixture. Stir in the coconut milk, raisins, chopped pineapple, and cashew nuts.

4. Pile the rice mixture into the pineapple shells. Wrap the pineapple leaves in foil to prevent them from burning and place on a cookie sheet. Bake in a preheated 325°F oven for 20 minutes.

TIME Preparation takes 20 minutes and cooking takes about 25 minutes.

Makes 1 Small Loaf

Irish Soda Bread

TRADITIONALLY THE IRISH ARE DAILY BAKERS
AND THIS IS THEIR EVERYDAY BREAD.

Ingredients

2 cups all-purpose flour

½ tsp salt

1 tsp bicarbonate of soda
(baking soda)

½ tsp cream of tartar

1 tbsp butter

¾ cup buttermilk

1. Mix the flour, salt, bicarbonate of soda, and cream of tartar together in a bowl, then cut in the butter.

2. Pour in the buttermilk and mix to a soft dough with a metal spatula. Turn out onto a floured surface and shape into a round—do not knead the dough.

3. Place on a floured baking sheet and score a cross in the top of the loaf using a sharp knife. Sprinkle lightly with flour.

4. Bake in a preheated 425°F oven for 10 minutes. Reduce the temperature to 400°F and bake for another 10 minutes. Cool on a wire rack.

TIME Preparation takes 10 to 15 minutes and cooking takes about 20 minutes.

COOK'S TIP To make a light soda bread, it is important to mix it as quickly and lightly as possible.

Serves 6

Sri Lankan Rice

SERVE THIS RICE DISH HOT AS AN ACCOMPANIMENT
TO VEGETABLE CURRIES OR PULSE DISHES.

Ingredients

2 tbsps sunflower oil

1 small onion, finely chopped

1 clove garlic, minced

½ tsp ground cumin

½ tsp ground coriander

½ tsp paprika

1 tsp turmeric

Large pinch of chili or
cayenne pepper

½ cup Basmati rice, washed
and drained

1¼ cups skim milk

½ tsp salt

Freshly ground black pepper
to taste

½ cup snow peas, trimmed
and cut in half

½ cup sliced mushrooms

¼ cup corn

¼ cup golden raisins, washed
and soaked

1. Heat the oil in a large nonstick saucepan. Add the onion and garlic and fry gently for 4 to 5 minutes.

2. Add the cumin, coriander, paprika, turmeric, and chili, and fry for another 3 to 4 minutes—do not allow the mixture to burn.

3. Add the washed rice and mix well with the onions and spices for about 2 minutes.

4. Add the milk and salt and pepper, stir gently, and bring to a boil. Cover the pan and simmer until all the liquid is absorbed and the rice is cooked, approximately 15 to 20 minutes.

5. While the rice is cooking, steam the snow peas, mushrooms, corn, and golden raisins. Fold the vegetables into the rice.

6. Serve immediately or transfer to a serving dish to cool.

TIME Preparation takes 15 minutes and cooking takes about 25 minutes.

Right: Sri Lankan Rice

Serves 6

Refried Beans

BEANS ARE ONE OF MEXICO'S MOST IMPORTANT
INGREDIENTS, AND REFRIED BEANS IS A CLASSIC
ACCOMPANIMENT TO NUMEROUS MEXICAN AND
TEX-MEX MAIN COURSES.

Ingredients

1¼ cups dried pinto beans

Water to cover

1 bay leaf

6 tbsps oil

Salt and freshly ground
black pepper

Grated mild cheese

Shredded lettuce

Tortillas

TIME Preparation takes about
15 minutes. The beans must be
soaked overnight or rehydrated by
the quick method. They must be
cooked at least 2 hours before
frying.

1. Soak the beans overnight. Change the water, add the bay leaf, and bring to a boil. Cover and simmer about 2 hours, or until the beans are completely tender. Alternatively, bring the beans to a boil in cold water and then allow to boil rapidly for 10 minutes. Cover and leave to stand for one hour. Change the water and then continue with the recipe. Drain the beans and reserve a small amount of the cooking liquid. Discard the bay leaf.

2. Heat the oil in a heavy skillet. Add the beans and, as they fry, mash them with the back of a spoon. Do not over-mash; about a third of the beans should stay whole. Season to taste.

3. Smooth out the beans in the pan and cook until the bottom is set but not browned. Turn the beans over and cook the other side.

4. Top with the cheese and cook the beans until the cheese melts. Serve with finely shredded lettuce and tortillas, either warm or cut in triangles and deep-fried until crisp.

Serves 4

Roasted Vegetables

THE FLAVORS AND COLORS OF CRISP MEDITERRANEAN-STYLE VEGETABLES
ARE COMBINED IN THIS DELICIOUS AND NUTRITIOUS RECIPE.

Ingredients

1 Spanish or red onion, sliced

1 white or yellow onion, sliced

4 zucchini, thickly sliced

8 ounces baby corn

1 eggplant, cut into chunks

1 red bell pepper, cored and
cut into large dice

1 yellow bell pepper, cored
and cut into large dice

2 cloves garlic, thinly sliced

4 tsps olive oil

Salt and freshly ground
black pepper

2-3 tbsps chopped fresh
mixed herbs

TIME Preparation takes
10 minutes and cooking takes
20 to 30 minutes.

1. Place all the vegetables and garlic in a
nonstick roasting pan and mix together.

2. Add the oil and seasoning and toss
until the vegetables are lightly coated
with oil.

3. Bake in a preheated oven at 425°F for

20 to 30 minutes, until just tender and
tinged brown at the edges. Stir once or
twice during cooking.

4. Sprinkle with the herbs and toss to
mix. Serve hot or cold.

Serves 6

Noodles with Poppy Seeds and Raisins

CHRISTMAS EVE DINNER IN POLAND TRADITIONALLY HAD
UP TO 21 COURSES, OF WHICH THIS WAS BUT ONE!

Ingredients

8 ounces noodles or
other pasta shapes

Pinch of salt

1 tbsp oil

½ cup heavy cream

6 tbsps black poppy seeds,
ground

2 tbsps honey

6 tbsps raisins

1. Bring lots of water to a boil in a large
saucepan with a pinch of salt. Add the
oil and the noodles or other pasta
shapes and bring back to a boil. Cook,
uncovered, for about 10 to 12 minutes
until tender.

2. Drain the pasta and rinse under hot
water. If using immediately, allow to
drain dry. If not, place in a bowl of
water to keep.

3. Place the heavy cream in a deep,
heavy-based saucepan and bring almost
to a boil.

4. When the cream reaches the scalding
point, mix in the poppy seeds, honey,
and raisins. Cook slowly for about
5 minutes, or until the mixture
becomes thick but will still fall off a
spoon easily.

5. Toss the poppy seed mixture with the
noodles and serve hot.

TIME Preparation takes about 15 minutes
and cooking takes about 15 minutes.

Makes One Loaf

Roman Focaccia

THIS CLASSIC ITALIAN BREAD IS TOPPED WITH THINLY SLICED
RAW ONION THAT BAKES TO A GOLDEN BROWN IN THE OVEN.

Ingredients

1 ounce compressed yeast

1 cup lukewarm water

4 cups bread flour or
all-purpose flour

1 tsp salt

⅓ cup fruity olive oil

2 large onions

1 large sprig fresh rosemary

Coarse sea salt

1. Crumble the yeast into the warm water, leave for 3 to 4 minutes, then stir to completely dissolve the yeast.

2. Mix the flour and salt together and make a well in the center. Add ¼ cup of the olive oil and the yeast liquid, and mix together into a manageable dough.

3. Turn out onto a lightly floured surface and knead until smooth and elastic. Return the dough to the bowl, cover, and leave in a warm place until doubled in bulk—about 1 hour.

4. Slice the onions very thinly and place in cold water. Leave to soak for at least 30 minutes.

5. Punch the dough down and roll it out to fit an oiled baking pan about 16 x 10 inches. Lift the dough into the pan, pressing it well into the corners. Cover and leave in a warm place to rise for 20 to 30 minutes. Drain the onion slices and dry thoroughly.

6. Brush the dough with the remaining oil then top with the onion slices. Strip the rosemary leaves from the stalk and chop finely. Scatter them over the onions with some coarse sea salt.

7. Bake in a preheated 425°F oven for 20 to 30 minutes, until the onions are soft and the bread is a pale golden brown. Cool on a wire rack.

VARIATION Sprinkle ¼ cup freshly grated Parmesan over the onion topping before baking.

TIME Preparation takes about 2¼ hours and cooking takes 20 to 30 minutes.

Makes 18 Small Breads

Pita Bread

THESE ARE THE BEST KNOWN OF ALL THE FLAT BREADS. THEY ARE EATEN
THROUGHOUT THE MEDITERRANEAN WITH DIPS AND BARBECUED MEATS.

Ingredients

½ ounce compressed yeast

1¼ cups lukewarm water

4 cups all-purpose flour

½ tsp salt

1. Crumble the yeast into half the water and stir until completely dissolved. Leave in a warm place, loosely covered, until the yeast bubbles—about 20 minutes.

2. Mix the flour and salt in a bowl and gradually add the yeast mixture. Stir with a wooden spoon while adding the rest of the water to form a stiff dough.

3. Knead the dough until it is smooth and elastic. Divide the dough into 18 pieces, cover, and leave in a warm place for 30 minutes.

4. Roll out each piece of dough on a floured board to form a thin round. Sprinkle lightly with more flour, cover, and leave for 1 hour.

5. Flatten the rounds and roll out again, then cover and leave for another 30 minutes.

6. Bake the pita breads in batches on a floured baking sheet at the top of a preheated 500°F oven for about 10 minutes; they will puff up but will flatten immediately when removed from the oven.

TIME Preparation takes about 3 hours and cooking takes 10 minutes per batch.

COOK'S TIP Do not allow the pitas to brown too much during baking—they should be only slightly browned.

VARIATION Use the dough to make just 12 breads if you prefer your pitas slightly thicker.

Makes 8

Naan Bread

THESE BREADS FROM INDIA ARE TRADITIONALLY COOKED IN A CLAY OVEN CALLED A
TANDOOR, BUT A VERY HOT CONVENTIONAL OVEN WILL DO JUST AS WELL.

Ingredients

4 cups all-purpose flour

1 tsp salt

1 tsp sugar

⅓ cup milk

1 ounce compressed yeast

¼ cup butter

⅔ cup plain yogurt

1 large egg, beaten

2 tbsps sesame seeds
or poppy seeds

TIME Preparation takes 1¼ to
2 hours and cooking takes about
10 minutes.

VARIATION Mix minced garlic
and freshly chopped cilantro into
the yogurt before glazing the
naan breads.

1. Place the flour, salt, and sugar in a large bowl, and mix together well.

2. Heat the milk until it is lukewarm, crumble in the yeast, and leave for 3 to 4 minutes before stirring until the yeast is completely dissolved. Melt the butter, then leave it until it is just lukewarm.

3. Add the yeast liquid, all but 1 tbsp of the yogurt, the egg, and melted butter to the flour. Mix to a soft dough, turn out onto a floured surface, and knead until soft and elastic.

4. Place the dough in a clean bowl, cover and leave in a warm place for about 1 hour, until doubled in bulk.

5. Divide the dough into 8 balls, kneading them lightly then cover and leave for 10 to 15 minutes.

6. Place two ungreased baking sheets in a preheated 450°F oven for about 10 minutes to heat through. Remove the hot baking sheets from the oven and flour them lightly.

7. Shape the balls by stretching or rolling into teardrop shapes about 6 to 7

inches long. Place on the baking sheets, brush with the reserved yogurt, and sprinkle with the sesame seeds or poppy seeds.

8. Bake one sheet at a time on the top shelf of the oven for about 10 minutes, or until puffed and browned.

Serves 6

Ratatouille

THIS DELICIOUS VEGETABLE CASSEROLE FROM THE SOUTH OF FRANCE
HAS BECOME A GREAT FAVORITE ACROSS THE WORLD.

Ingredients

5 tbsps olive oil

2 Spanish or red onions,
thinly sliced

2 green or red bell peppers,
cored and coarsely chopped

4 zucchini, thickly sliced

2 eggplants, coarsely chopped

2 x 1 pound 12 ounce cans
of peeled plum tomatoes

1 large clove garlic, minced

2½ tsps chopped fresh basil

Salt and freshly ground
black pepper

⅔ cup dry white wine

1. Heat the oil in a large saucepan, add the onion slices, and fry for 5 minutes until they are soft and just beginning to brown.

2. Stir in the bell peppers and zucchini, and cook gently for 5 minutes until they begin to soften. Remove all the vegetables from the pan and set them aside.

3. Put the chopped eggplant into the saucepan with the vegetable juices. Cook gently until it begins to brown.

4. Add the cans of tomatoes, garlic, and basil to the saucepan along with the sautéed vegetables, mixing well to blend in evenly. Bring to a boil, then reduce the heat and simmer for 15 minutes, or until the liquid in the pan reduces and thickens.

5. Add the seasoning and wine to the pan and continue cooking for a further 15 minutes, before serving straight away, or chilling and serving cold.

COOK'S TIP If the liquid in the pan is still thin and excessive after the full cooking time, remove the vegetables and boil the juices rapidly until they have reduced and thickened.

TIME Preparation takes 20 minutes, plus 30 minutes standing time. Cooking takes about 35 minutes.

Zucchini *A member of the squash family, zucchini are picked young and are smaller than many of their cousins. Most varieties are dark green in color, although both a variegated and a yellow variety are also available. Zucchini flowers are occasionally sold and these edible blossoms are delightful stuffed and baked.*

Serves 4–6

Cardamom Rice

THE DELICATE FLAVOR OF THIS INDIAN RICE DISH MAKES IT
SUITABLE FOR SERVING WITH A WHOLE HOST OF DISHES.

Ingredients

1½ cups basmati rice

4 tbsps ghee or unsalted butter

6 green cardamoms,
split open on the top

1 tsp black cumin seeds or
caraway seeds

1 tsp salt or to taste

2¼ cups water

TIME Preparation takes 5 to 10 minutes plus time needed to soak the rice; cooking takes 20 to 25 minutes.

1. Wash the rice, soak in cold water for ½ to 1 hour and drain thoroughly.

2. Melt the ghee or butter over low heat and fry the cardamom and caraway seeds for 1 minute.

3. Add the rice, stir and fry over medium heat for 2 to 3 minutes. Adjust heat to low, stir and fry for another 2 to 3 minutes.

4. Add salt and water and mix well. Bring to a boil, cover the pan, and simmer for 12 minutes, without lifting the lid.

5. Remove from heat and leave the pot undisturbed for 6 to 8 minutes before serving.

COOK'S TIP Do not lift the lid or stir the rice during cooking. Do not stir immediately after the rice has been cooked.

Serves 4

Eggplant and Pepper Szechuan Style

AUTHENTIC SZECHUAN FOOD IS FIERY HOT. OUTSIDE CHINA,
RESTAURANTS OFTEN TONE DOWN THE TASTE FOR WESTERN PALATES.

Ingredients

Oil for frying

1 large eggplant, cubed

2 cloves garlic, minced

*1-inch piece fresh ginger root,
peeled and shredded*

1 onion, cut into 1-inch pieces

*1 small green bell pepper, cored
and cut into 1-inch pieces*

*1 small red bell pepper, cored
and cut into 1-inch pieces*

*1 red or green chili, cored
and cut into thin strips*

½ cup vegetable broth

1 tsp sugar

1 tsp vinegar

*Pinch of salt and freshly
ground black pepper*

1 tsp cornstarch

1 tbsp soy sauce

Dash of sesame oil

Oil for cooking

TIME Preparation takes about 30 minutes
and cooking takes 7 to 8 minutes.

1. Heat about 3 tbsps oil in a wok. Add the eggplant and stir-fry 4 to 5 minutes. It may be necessary to add more oil as the eggplant cooks. Remove from the wok and set aside.

2. Reheat the wok and add 2 tbsps oil. Add the garlic and ginger root and stir-fry for 1 minute. Add the onion and stir-fry for 2 minutes. Add the bell pepper and chili and stir-fry for 1 minute. Return the eggplant to the wok along with the remaining ingredients.

3. Bring to a boil, stirring constantly, and cook until the sauce thickens and clears. Serve immediately.

Eggplant *The eggplant is thought to
have originated in India, from where it spread
gradually to other warm regions. It is basically a
large berry which can vary in shape from oblong to
round, and in color from white to deep purple.
When choosing an eggplant, pick the small fruit,
which have a superior taste.*

The World Vegetarian Cookbook 115

Serves 4

Stir-fried Sticky Rice

THE CHINESE SERVE THEIR RICE STICKY—THIS NOT
ONLY GIVES IT A LOVELY TEXTURE, BUT ALSO MAKES
IT EASIER TO EAT WITH CHOPSTICKS.

Ingredients

1¼ cups glutinous rice

2 tbsps vegetable oil

2 green onions,
chopped

½ onion, chopped

1 slice fresh ginger root

4 dried Chinese black
mushrooms, soaked for
15 minutes in warm water,
drained and sliced

Salt and freshly ground
black pepper

TIME Preparation takes
5 minutes and cooking takes
approximately 25 minutes.

1. Wash the rice in plenty of cold water and place it in a sieve. Pour 5½ cups of boiling water over the rice.

2. Heat the oil in a wok and fry the green onions, onion, and ginger root until golden brown. Add the mushrooms and continue cooking, stirring and shaking the wok frequently.

3. Add the rice and stir well. Pour over enough water to cover the rice by about ½ inch.

4. Cover and cook over a moderate heat until there is almost no liquid left. Reduce the heat once again and continue cooking until all the liquid has been absorbed. This takes about 20 minutes. Add salt and pepper to taste, remove the slice of ginger root and serve immediately.

Right: Stir-fried Sticky Rice

Leeks Provençal

A BASIC PROVENÇAL SAUCE OF TOMATOES, GARLIC,
AND HERBS GOES WELL WITH MOST SAVORY DISHES.
WITH LEEKS IT IS EXCEPTIONAL.

Ingredients

6 leeks, washed and trimmed

Salt

1 tbsp olive oil

2 cloves garlic, minced

4 tomatoes, peeled, seeded,
and chopped

1 tsp dried thyme

2 tbsps chopped fresh parsley

4 tbsps dry white wine

Freshly ground black pepper

Sprigs of fresh parsley
to garnish

1. Cut the leeks into 2-inch pieces and cook for 10 to 15 minutes in lightly salted boiling water, until tender.

2. Heat the oil in a small saucepan and fry the garlic until softened, but not browned. Stir in the tomatoes, herbs, and wine, and simmer gently for 10 minutes until the tomatoes are soft. Season with salt and pepper.

3. Drain the cooked leeks and place in a serving dish with the tomato mixture. Toss to mix. Serve garnished with a sprig of parsley.

TIME Preparation takes about
10 minutes and cooking takes
25 minutes.

Serves 4–6

Long Beans in Coconut Milk

IN THIS THAI RECIPE, THE LONG BEANS ARE LIGHTLY COOKED
AND SHOULD STILL BE SLIGHTLY CRUNCHY WHEN SERVED.

Ingredients

1 pound long beans

1 tbsp oil

2 stems lemongrass, sliced

1-inch piece galangal, sliced
into thin sticks

1 large red chili, seeded and
chopped

1¼ cups thin coconut milk

Chili "flowers" to garnish

1. Top and tail the beans and cut into
   2-inch pieces.

2. Heat the oil in a wok and stir-fry the
   lemongrass, galangal, and chili for
   1 minute. Add the coconut milk and
   bring to a boil. Boil for 3 minutes.

3. Stir in the beans, reduce the heat, and
   simmer for 6 minutes. Garnish with
   chili "flowers" (see below) and serve
   immediately.

TIME Preparation takes 10 minutes and
cooking takes 7 minutes.

Red Chilies *Red chilies are used extensively in
Asian cooking, both as an ingredient and as a garnish. Chili
flowers, a popular garnish, are made by slicing the chili from
stem to tip and soaking it in ice water until the strips
curl. As well as being used fresh, chilies are
also dried to preserve them and
intensify their flavor.*

Serves 4 – 6

Saag Bhaji

SPINACH ADOPTS OTHER FLAVORS WELL. HERE, A DELICIOUS RESULT IS OBTAINED BY SIMMERING IT IN SPICES AND THEN COMBINING IT WITH DICED, FRIED POTATOES.

Ingredients

½ cup cooking oil

½ tsp mustard seeds

1 tsp cumin seeds

8-10 fenugreek seeds (optional)

1 tbsp curry leaves or
1 tsp curry powder

2-3 cloves garlic, finely chopped

2-4 dried red chilies,
coarsely chopped

1 pound fresh leaf spinach
or 8 ounces frozen leaf spinach,
finely chopped

1 tbsp ghee or unsalted butter

1 large potato, peeled and diced

1 large onion, finely sliced

½ tsp ground turmeric

1 tsp ground cumin

½ tsp garam masala

¼-½ tsp chili powder

2-3 ripe tomatoes, peeled
and chopped

1 tsp salt or to taste

1. Heat 2 tbsps oil from the specified amount over medium heat and fry the mustard seeds until they pop. Add the cumin seeds, fenugreek (if using), and curry leaves or powder, and immediately follow with the garlic and chili peppers. Allow garlic to turn slightly brown.

2. Add the spinach, stir and mix thoroughly. Cover and simmer for 15 minutes, stirring occasionally.

3. Melt the ghee or butter over medium heat and brown the diced potatoes. Remove from heat and set aside.

4. Heat the remaining oil over medium heat and fry the onions until well browned, about 10 minutes. Do not burn the onions or they will taste bitter.

5. Turn the heat down to minimum and add the turmeric, cumin, garam masala, and chili powder. Stir and fry for 2 to 3 minutes.

6. Add the spinach, potatoes, tomatoes, and salt. Cover and simmer for 10 minutes or until the potatoes are tender, stirring occasionally. Remove from heat and serve.

TIME Preparation takes 25 to 30 minutes and cooking takes 50 minutes.

Serves 4

Stir-fried Chinese Cabbage

CHINESE CABBAGE IS FLAVORED WITH SESAME OIL
AND SOY SAUCE IN THIS ZINGY DISH.

Ingredients

2 zucchini

2 tbsps vegetable oil

5 cups Chinese cabbage,
finely shredded

1 tsp chopped garlic

1 tbsp chopped red chili

1 tbsp soy sauce

Salt and freshly ground
pepper

Few tsps sesame oil

1. Prepare the zucchini, first topping and tailing them and then slicing down the sides, preserving a bit of the flesh with the peel. Slice finely.

2. Heat the oil in a wok, add the Chinese cabbage and garlic, and stir-fry for 2 minutes.

3. Add the zucchini, chili, soy sauce, salt, and pepper. Continue cooking for 3 minutes and serve hot with the sesame oil drizzled on top.

PREPARATION Cooked in this way, the Chinese cabbage will remain crisp. If you prefer, cook longer for a softer texture.

VARIATION If you like hot, spicy dishes, add ¼ tsp chili sauce to the Chinese cabbage.

TIME Preparation takes about 10 minutes and cooking takes 5 minutes.

Right: Stir-fried Chinese Cabbage

Turkish Pilaf

TURKEY IS FAMOUS FOR ITS APRICOTS, GOLDEN
RAISINS, AND PISTACHIO NUTS. THIS RECIPE MAKES
GOOD USE OF THEM ALL.

Ingredients

2½ tbsps oil

2 cups long-grain rice

1 quart water

½ tsp salt

¼ cup split blanched almonds

¼ cup shelled pistachio nuts

¼ cup golden raisins

¼ cup chopped dried
apricots

TIME Preparation takes 10 to 15 minutes and cooking takes about 20 minutes.

SERVING IDEA Decorate with sprigs of fresh greens, such as cilantro leaves, watercress, or mâche.

1. Heat 2 tablespoons of the oil in a large saucepan over high heat. Add the rice and cook, stirring constantly with a wooden spoon, until all the grains are coated.

2. Add water and salt and cover the pan with a cloth, then with the lid. Reduce the heat to a simmer and cook for 15 minutes.

3. Meanwhile, toast the almonds in a dry, nonstick skillet. When they start to give off their characteristic aroma (after about 5 minutes), they are ready.

4. Remove the rice from the heat; it should have absorbed all the liquid. If not, return rice to the heat, uncovered, for a few minutes to finish evaporation. Transfer rice to a large bowl and stir in the almonds, pistachios, raisins, and apricots.

5. Serve the rice heaped in a mound on a serving platter, or press it into a ring mold brushed with oil, then unmold to give rice an attractive shape on a platter.

Serves 4–6

Potatoes with Garlic and Chilies

THESE ARE RATHER LIKE A SPICY INDIAN VERSION
OF FRENCH FRIES, BUT THEY ARE NOT DEEP-FRIED.

Ingredients

3-4 potatoes, peeled
and washed

3 tbsps cooking oil

½ tsp mustard seeds

½ tsp cumin seeds

4 cloves garlic, minced

¼-½ tsp chili powder

½ tsp ground turmeric

1 tsp salt or to taste

1. Cut the potatoes to the thickness of French fries, but half their length.

2. In a large nonstick or cast-iron skillet, heat the oil over medium heat. Add the mustard seeds and then the cumin. When the seeds start popping, add the garlic and allow it to turn lightly brown.

3. Remove the pan from the heat and add the chili powder and turmeric. Add the potatoes and place the pan back on heat. Stir and turn heat up to medium.

4. Add the salt, stir and mix, cover the pan, cook for 3 to 4 minutes and stir again. Continue to do this until the potatoes are cooked and lightly browned. Remove from the heat.

TIME Preparation takes 15 to 20 minutes and cooking takes 15 minutes.

VARIATION Use cauliflower, cut into small flowerets, instead of potato.

Potatoes *Among the most widely cultivated vegetables, the potato is one of the world's most important staples. Easily grown and highly nutritious (it contains elements such as copper and iron, vitamin C, thiamin, riboflavin, and pantothenic acid, and is low in salts), it is cultivated on every continent and virtually every country has a plethora of recipes that include it.*

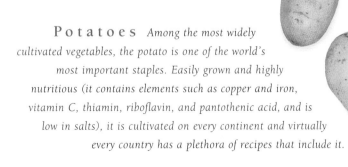

Makes 12

Wheat-flour Tortillas

THESE MEXICAN UNLEAVENED FLAT BREADS ARE MADE WITH WHEAT FLOUR AND ARE
EASIER TO PREPARE THAN THE MORE AUTHENTIC CORN VARIETY.

Ingredients

4 cups all-purpose flour

1 tbsp salt

Scant ⅓ cup shortening

1¼ cups hot water

TIME Preparation takes 20 to 25 minutes and cooking takes about 5 minutes.

COOK'S TIP Do not overcook tortillas; they must be pliable or they will crack when rolled around a filling.

1. Mix the flour and salt together in a bowl then cut in the shortening until the mixture resembles bread crumbs. Gradually add the water to form a soft, pliable dough.

2. Knead the dough on a well-floured surface until smooth and no longer sticky. Divide the dough into 12 pieces, keeping the dough that is not being worked covered to prevent it from drying out.

3. Knead each piece into a ball, then roll out each ball into a very thin circle, using a floured rolling pin. Cut into neat rounds using a 10-inch plate as a guide.

4. Stack the tortillas as you make them, flouring each one well to prevent them from sticking together. Cover with a clean cloth.

5. Heat a heavy-based skillet until evenly hot, and carefully add a tortilla. Cook

for about 10 seconds per side. Stack and keep covered until all are cooked. Use according to your chosen recipe.

Makes 1 Large Loaf

English Cottage Milk Loaf

BREADS WITH MILK HAVE A MUCH SOFTER CRUST THAN THOSE MADE WITH WATER.
THIS IS IDEAL FOR COTTAGE LOAVES AS IT MAKES THEM EASIER TO SLICE.

Ingredients

½ ounce compressed yeast

Scant 2 cups lukewarm milk

*6 cups bread flour or
all-purpose flour*

1 tsp salt

¼ cup butter

Beaten egg to glaze

Poppy seeds

TIME Preparation takes about
2 hours and cooking takes
30 to 35 minutes.

COOK'S TIP Ensure you seal
the topknot on firmly.

1. Crumble the yeast into half the milk
   and leave for 3 to 4 minutes, then stir
   to completely dissolve the yeast.

2. Mix the flour and salt together, and cut
   in the butter. Make a well in the center
   and pour in the yeast liquid. Mix to a
   soft but manageable dough, adding as
   much of the remaining milk as
   necessary.

3. Turn out onto a lightly-floured surface
   and knead thoroughly until smooth and
   elastic. Return the dough to the bowl,
   cover and leave in a warm place for
   45 to 60 minutes, until doubled in bulk.

4. Punch the dough down and divide into
   two, one piece being about double the
   size of the other.

5. Shape the larger piece of dough into a
   round loaf and place it on a floured
   baking sheet. Shape the small piece into a
   round and place it on top. Flour your
   index finger, or the handle of a wooden
   spoon, and press it firmly through the
   center of the topknot, down to the
   baking sheet, to seal the two together.
   Cover loosely and leave in a warm place
   for about 30 minutes, until the loaf is
   well risen.

6. Brush the loaf with beaten egg and
   sprinkle some poppy seeds over the top
   of the loaf. Bake in a preheated 425°F
   oven for 30 to 35 minutes, until the loaf
   sounds hollow when tapped underneath.
   Transfer to a wire rack to cool.

Serves 4 – 6

Carrot Pilau

PLAIN BOILED RICE IS TRANSFORMED INTO A COLORFUL
AND FLAVORFUL PILAU IN THIS AROMATIC DISH.

Ingredients

1¼ cups basmati rice,
washed and soaked in cold
water for ½ hour

2¼ cups water

1 tsp salt or to taste

1 tsp butter

2 tbsps ghee or unsalted butter

1 tsp cumin or caraway seeds

1 onion, finely sliced

2 cinnamon sticks, 2-inches
long, broken up

4 green cardamoms, split open

1 tsp garam masala or ground
mixed spice

¾ cup coarsely grated carrots

⅔ cup frozen peas

½ tsp salt or to taste

TIME Preparation takes about
15 minutes, plus time needed to
soak the rice. Cooking takes
25 to 30 minutes.

1. Drain the rice thoroughly and put into a saucepan with the water. Bring to a boil, and stir in the salt and 1 tsp butter. Boil steadily for 1 minute.

2. Place the lid on the saucepan and simmer for 12 to 15 minutes. Do not lift the lid during cooking.

3. Remove the pan from heat and keep it covered for another 10 minutes.

4. Meanwhile, prepare the rest of the ingredients. Melt the ghee or butter over medium heat, add the cumin or caraway seeds, and fry until they crackle.

5. Add the onion, cinnamon, and cardamom, and fry until the onions are lightly browned, about 4 to 5 minutes, stirring frequently.

6. Add the garam masala or ground mixed spice. Stir and cook for 30 seconds. Add the carrots, peas, and salt, stir and then cook for 1 to 2 minutes.

7. Now add the rice, stir, and mix gently using a metal spoon or a fork as a wooden spoon or spatula will squash the grains. Remove the pan from heat and serve.

Carrots *The carrot has been cultivated since about 500 BC, and over the centuries the sweet and savory characteristics of this extremely adaptable vegetable have resulted in it being used in everything from drinks to cakes. On the health side, carrots are rich in vitamins, particularly vitamin A.*

DESSERTS

Obviously, choosing a dessert poses far fewer problems for the vegetarian than other courses, and their inclusion in a vegetarian book may seem a little unnecessary. The choice of desserts in this section, however, is designed to complement our main courses without any of those hidden surprises, such as gelatin. As you would expect, many of the best desserts from around the world are based on fruit. A simple fruit salad is one of the most healthful desserts, and we have included a few variations on this theme. These are great for everyday meals but, if something just that little bit special is called for, try Raspberry Soufflé, Coconut and Banana Pancakes, or Spiced Mango Fool. If it's a taste of the exotic you crave, indulge in Vermicelli Kheer, or a delicious Kompot.

Serves 4

Spun Fruits

OFTEN CALLED TOFFEE FRUITS, THIS CHINESE SWEET CONSISTS OF FRUIT
FRIED IN BATTER AND COATED WITH A THIN, CRISP CARAMEL GLAZE.

Ingredients

Oil for deep frying

Batter

1 cup all-purpose flour, sifted

Pinch of salt

1 egg

*½ cup water and milk,
mixed half and half*

Caramel syrup

1 cup sugar

3 tbsps water

1 tbsp oil

*1 large apple, peeled, cored, and
cut into 2-inch chunks*

*1 banana, peeled and cut
into 1-inch pieces*

Ice water

1. Combine all the batter ingredients in a food processor or blender and process to blend. Pour into a bowl and dip in the prepared fruit.

2. In a heavy-based pan, combine the sugar with the water and oil, and cook over very low heat until the sugar dissolves. Bring to a boil and boil rapidly until a pale caramel color.

3. While the sugar is dissolving, heat the oil in a wok or saucepan and fry the battered fruit, a few pieces at a time.

4. While the fruit is still hot and crisp, use chopsticks or a pair of tongs to dip the fruit into the hot caramel syrup. Stir each piece around to coat evenly.

5. Dip immediately into ice water to harden the syrup, and place each piece on a greased dish. Continue cooking all the fruit in the same way.

6. Once the caramel has hardened and the fruit has cooled, transfer to a clean serving plate.

TIME Preparation takes 25 minutes and cooking takes 10 to 15 minutes.

COOK'S TIP Watch the syrup carefully and do not allow it to become too brown, as this will give the dish a bitter taste.

Serves 6

Raspberry Soufflé

THE AUTHENTIC VERSION OF THIS ENTICING IRISH RECIPE FEATURES GELATIN.
A VEGETARIAN SUBSTITUTE—AGAR FLAKES—IS USED HERE.

Ingredients

1 pound raspberries (frozen raspberries, thawed, can be used)

½ cup superfine sugar

4 eggs, separated

¼ cup confectioners' sugar

2 tbsps agar flakes

1¼ cups heavy cream, lightly whipped

Mint sprigs to decorate

TIME Preparation takes about 1 hour.

1. Tie a greased piece of wax paper around a 6-inch soufflé dish to form a collar above the rim of the dish.

2. Reserve a few of the raspberries and strain the rest through a sieve. Fold the superfine sugar into the raspberry purée.

4. Whip the egg yolks and confectioner's sugar together over the hot water. Fold in the raspberry purée and cool. Fold in half the cream and the agar flakes, mixing thoroughly.

5. Whip the egg whites until stiff, then fold into the mixture with a metal spoon. Turn into the prepared soufflé dish and chill to set.

6. When set, remove the collar and decorate the soufflé with the whipped cream, raspberries, and mint sprigs.

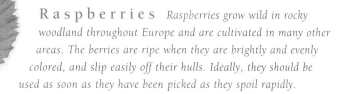

Raspberries *Raspberries grow wild in rocky woodland throughout Europe and are cultivated in many other areas. The berries are ripe when they are brightly and evenly colored, and slip easily off their hulls. Ideally, they should be used as soon as they have been picked as they spoil rapidly.*

Serves 4

Coconut and Banana Pancakes

THIS UNUSUAL DESSERT FROM THAILAND
CAN BE SERVED WARM OR COLD.

Ingredients

½ cup rice flour

Pinch of salt

2 eggs

1½ cups thin coconut milk

Green food coloring (optional)

2 tbsps unsweetened shredded coconut

Oil for frying

Filling

2 tbsps lime juice

Grated rind of ½ lime

1 tsp sugar

1 tbsp unsweetened shredded coconut

2 bananas

1. Place the flour and the salt in a mixing bowl and make a well in the center. Drop the eggs and a little of the coconut milk into the well.

2. Using a wooden spoon, beat well, slowly incorporating the flour until you have a smooth, thick paste.

3. Gradually beat in the remaining coconut milk. Stir in a few drops of food coloring, if using. Allow to stand for 20 minutes.

4. Meanwhile, make the filling. Mix together the lime juice, rind, sugar, and 1 tbsp coconut. Slice the bananas and toss them in the mixture.

5. Stir the 2 tbsps coconut into the pancake batter. Heat a little oil in an 8-inch heavy-based skillet. Pour off the excess and spoon in about 4 tbsps of the batter. Swirl to coat the pan. Cook for about 1 minute, or until the underside is golden.

6. Flip or toss the pancake over and cook the other side. Slide the pancake out of the pan and keep warm. Repeat until all the batter is used. Fill the pancakes with the banana mixture and serve immediately.

SERVING IDEA Fold the pancakes into quarters and spoon some filling inside, or divide filling between the pancakes and roll up.

TIME Preparation takes 15 minutes, plus 20 minutes standing time. Cooking takes 15 minutes.

Bananas *Alexander the Great is known to have come across bananas on his travels to India and subsequently, thanks to explorers and conquerors, the banana plant spread throughout the tropical world. In Europe and temperate America, however, they remained virtually unknown until the 1890s, when the first refrigerated ships were able to transport them over long distances.*

Serves 6–8

Key Lime Pie

THE FLORIDA KEYS ARE HOME TO THIS DELIGHTFULLY
SHARP AND REFRESHING DESSERT.

Ingredients

Crust

1½ cups graham cracker crumbs

½ cup sugar

½ cup butter or
margarine, melted

Filling

2 eggs

15 ounces sweetened
condensed milk

½ cup lime juice

¼ tsp salt

Topping

1 cup sour cream

⅓ cup sugar

⅛ tsp salt

Garnish

Graham cracker crumbs

Grated lime rind

1. First prepare the base by blending together the crust ingredients. Press the mixture firmly into a 9-inch pie plate. Bake in a preheated 350°F oven for 10 minutes.

2. To prepare the filling, beat the eggs and milk together, and add the lime juice and salt. Pour the filling into the prepared crust and bake at 350°F for 10 minutes, or until set.

3. Meanwhile, prepare the topping by combining the sour cream, sugar, and salt. When the filling has set, spread the topping over the pie. Bake at 425°F for 5 minutes to allow the topping to set. Garnish with cracker crumbs and lime rind, and serve cold.

TIME Preparation takes about 25 minutes and cooking takes 25 minutes.

Serves 6–8

Cassata

NO SWEET SELECTION IS COMPLETE WITHOUT ICE CREAM.
THE ITALIAN KIND IS RICH, CREAMY, AND JUSTLY FAMOUS.

Ingredients

Almond layer

2 eggs, separated

½ cup confectioners' sugar

½ cup heavy cream

½ tsp almond extract

Chocolate layer

2 eggs, separated

½ cup confectioners' sugar

½ cup heavy cream

2 ounces semi-sweet chocolate

2 tbsps unsweetened cocoa

1½ tbsps water

Fruit layer

1 cup heavy cream

2 tbsps maraschino or light rum

1 egg white

½ cup confectioners' sugar

½ cup candied fruit

1 ounce shelled, chopped pistachios

1. To prepare the almond layer, beat the egg whites until stiff peaks form, gradually beating in the confectioners' sugar, a spoonful at a time. Lightly beat the egg yolks and fold in the whites.

2. Whip the cream with the almond extract until soft peaks form, then fold into the egg mixture. Lightly oil an 8-inch round cake pan. Pour in the almond layer mixture and smooth over the top. Cover with plastic wrap and freeze until firm.

3. To prepare the chocolate layer, beat the egg whites until stiff peaks form, gradually beating in the confectioners' sugar, a spoonful at a time. Whip the cream until soft, then fold into the egg white mixture. Put the chocolate in the top of a double boiler over simmering water. Remove it from the heat and stir in the egg yolks. Combine cocoa and water and add to the chocolate mixture. Leave to cool and then fold into the egg white mixture. Spoon the chocolate layer over the almond layer and return, covered, to the freezer.

4. To make the rum fruit layer, whip the cream until soft peaks form. Whip the egg white until about the same consistency as cream. Gradually add the confectioners' sugar, beating well after each addition. Combine the two mixtures and fold in the rum, fruit, and nuts. Spread this mixture on top of the chocolate layer, cover, and freeze until firm.

5. To serve, loosen the cassata from around the edges of the pan with a small knife. Place a hot cloth around the pan for a few seconds to help loosen. Turn out onto a serving plate and cut into wedges to serve.

TIME Preparation takes several hours, so that one ice cream layer can freeze before another is added.

Serves 6

Tarte Tatin

THIS CLASSIC FRENCH "UPSIDE-DOWN" TART IS SAID
TO HAVE BEEN INVENTED BY ACCIDENT BY THE TWO
SISTERS TATIN IN THEIR HOTEL IN THE LOIRE.

Ingredients

⅓ cup butter

¾ cup sugar

2¼ pounds apples, peeled,
halved, and cored

1 pound flaky pastry

3 tbsps heavy cream

TIME Preparation takes about
15 minutes and cooking takes
30 minutes.

1. Dot the base of a medium pie pan
   with the butter and sprinkle with half
   the sugar.

2. Place the apple halves, rounded side
   down, onto the butter and sugar, and
   sprinkle over the remaining sugar.

3. Roll the pastry out into a round just
   slightly larger than the bottom of the
   pan. Place the pastry round over the
   apples, tucking it down at the edges.

4. Bake in a preheated 450°F oven for
   about 30 minutes. Remove from the
   oven when cooked and turn out
   immediately onto a serving plate.

5. Whip the cream and serve in a small
   bowl for guests to help themselves.

Apples *Of all the fruits that grow in the
temperate world, the apple is the undoubted king.
The Ancient Egyptians cultivated apple trees and
the Greeks and Romans knew them well. By the end of the
4th century AD, there were 37 varieties on record. From then on,
wherever Western civilization went, apples went too.*

Vermicelli Kheer

IN THIS POPULAR INDIAN DESSERT, THE VERMICELLI
IS LIGHTLY FRIED IN GHEE, THEN SIMMERED IN MILK
AND SPICES TO MAKE A RICH AND CREAMY DISH.

Ingredients

2 tbsps ghee or unsalted butter

10 ounces plain vermicelli

2 tbsps raisins

¼ cup almonds, blanched and
slivered

2½ cups whole milk

¼ cup sugar

1 tbsp ground almonds

½ tsp ground cardamom

½ tsp ground cinnamon

1 tbsp rose water, or 5-6 drops
of other flavorings such as
vanilla or almond

1. Melt the ghee or butter over low heat and add the vermicelli, raisins, and slivered almonds. Stir and fry for 2 to 3 minutes, until the vermicelli is golden brown.

2. Add the milk, sugar, and ground almonds, bring to a boil, and simmer gently for 20 minutes, stirring frequently.

3. Stir in the ground cardamom and cinnamon, and remove the pan from the heat.

4. Allow the kheer to cool slightly and stir in the rose water or other flavoring.

TIME Preparation takes 10 minutes and cooking takes 20 to 25 minutes.

Left: Tarte Tatin

Serves 6–8

Jamaican Mousse Cake

RUM, CHOCOLATE, AND BANANAS—TRUE TASTES OF THE CARIBBEAN—
ARE COMBINED IN THIS ENTICING DESSERT.

Ingredients

6 ounces semi-sweet chocolate

3 tbsps dark rum

1¼ cups heavy cream

2 large bananas, peeled
and mashed until smooth

1 tbsp light brown sugar

1 tbsp strong black coffee

3 eggs, separated

Chocolate curls to decorate

TIME Preparation takes about
30 minutes, plus chilling.

1. Break the chocolate into cubes and
place in a bowl over a pan of hot water,
or the top of a double boiler, to melt.
Once melted, stir in the rum and half of
the cream, beating well until smooth.

2. Put the mashed bananas, sugar, and
coffee in a large bowl, and beat until well
combined. Add the egg yolks and mix
well. Continue beating while adding all
the chocolate mixture.

3. Beat the egg whites until stiff and
forming peaks, then fold into the banana
mixture.

4. Spoon the mixture into a lightly greased
8-inch springform cake pan. Chill for at
least 2 hours, or until completely set and
firm.

5. Loosen the sides of the cake with a
warm knife, then remove the sides of
the pan. Carefully slide the cake off the
base of the pan onto a serving plate.

6. Whip the remaining cream and decorate
the cake with swirls of cream and
chocolate curls.

Serves 6–8

Spiced Mango Fool

IN INDIA, MANGO IS CONSIDERED TO BE THE KING OF ALL FRUITS. THE TASTE
OF THIS TROPICAL FRUIT IS A LITTLE LIKE A PEACH, BUT MUCH MORE EXOTIC.

Ingredients

2 tbsps milk

¼ tsp saffron strands

¾ cup evaporated milk

¼ cup sugar

1 level tbsp fine semolina or
cornmeal

2 heaping tbsps ground almonds

1 tsp ground cardamom

1 pound mango pulp, or
2 x 15-ounce cans of mangoes,
drained and puréed

1 cup thick-set plain yogurt

TIME Preparation takes
10 minutes and cooking takes
10 to 15 minutes.

1. Put the milk into a small saucepan and
bring to a boil. Stir in the saffron
strands, remove from the heat, cover
the pan, and set aside.

2. Put the evaporated milk and sugar into
a saucepan and place over a low heat.
When the milk begins to bubble,
sprinkle the semolina or cornmeal over
and stir until well blended.

3. Add the ground almonds, stir, and cook
until the mixture thickens—about
5 to 6 minutes.

4. Stir in the ground cardamom and
remove from the heat. Allow this to
cool completely, then gradually beat in
the mango pulp, making sure there are
no lumps.

5. In a large mixing bowl, beat the yogurt
with a fork. Gradually beat in the
evaporated milk and mango mixture.

6. Stir in the saffron milk, along with all
the strands for their color and flavor.
Mix well. Put the mango fool in a
serving dish and chill for 2 to 3 hours.

Strawberries *Today's large, succulent strawberries
would have been a revelation to our ancestors, whose wild
strawberries were much smaller. Big is not neccesarily beautiful,
however. One of the most flavorful varieties is the Alpine strawberry,
a miniature plant that produces fruit throughout the summer.*

Serves 4

Figs with Currants and Orange

FRUIT IS THE MOST POPULAR DESSERT IN GREECE,
AND FRESH FIGS ARE A FAVORITE CHOICE.

Ingredients

4 fresh figs

Small bunches of fresh redcurrants

6 oranges

1 tsp orange flower water

TIME Preparation takes about 15 minutes, plus chilling time.

1. Cut the stalks off the tops of the figs, but do not peel them. Cut the figs in quarters, but do not cut completely through the base. Open the figs out like flowers and stand them on their bases on serving dishes.

2. Arrange small bunches of redcurrants on the figs. Squeeze the juice from two of the oranges. Peel and segment the other four and arrange segments around each fig.

3. Mix the orange juice mixed with the orange flower water and pour over the figs. Chill before serving.

SERVING IDEAS Yogurt and honey may be served as an accompaniment.

Orange *China is thought to be the home of the sweet orange, which first found its way across Europe with the Romans. Its spread did not end there, however, and today there are huge orange groves in North Africa, Israel, Florida, and California.*

Mexican Chocolate Flan

FLAN IN MEXICO IS A MOLDED CUSTARD WITH A CARAMEL SAUCE.
CHOCOLATE AND CINNAMON IS A FAVORITE FLAVOR COMBINATION.

Ingredients

½ cup sugar

2 tbsps water

Juice of ½ a lemon

1 cup milk

2 ounces semi-sweet chocolate

1 cinnamon stick

2 whole eggs

2 egg yolks

4 tbsps sugar

1. Combine the ½ cup sugar with the water and lemon juice in a small, heavy-based saucepan.

2. Cook over gentle heat until the sugar starts to dissolve. Swirl the pan from time to time, but do not stir.

3. Once the sugar liquifies, bring the syrup to a boil and cook until golden brown.

4. While preparing the syrup, heat 4 custard cups in a 350°F oven. When the syrup is ready, pour into the cups and swirl to coat the sides and base evenly. Leave to cool at room temperature.

5. Chop the chocolate into small pieces and heat with the milk and cinnamon stick, stirring occasionally to help the chocolate dissolve.

6. Whip the whole eggs and the extra yolks together with the remaining sugar until slightly frothy. Gradually beat in the chocolate milk. Remove the cinnamon stick.

7. Pour the chocolate custard carefully into the custard cups and place them in a roasting pan of hand-hot water.

8. Place the roasting pan in the oven and bake the custards until just slightly wobbly in the center, about 20 to 30 minutes. Cool at room temperature and refrigerate for several hours, or overnight, before serving. Loosen the custards carefully from the sides of the dishes and invert onto serving plates. Shake to allow custard to drop out.

COOK'S TIP Do not allow custard to over-cook or it will form a tough skin on top. If the oven temperature is too high, it will cause the custard to boil and spoil the texture.

TIME Preparation takes about 30 minutes and cooking takes 35 to 40 minutes.

Serves 6

Caribbean Fruit Salad

THIS FRUIT SALAD IS MADE FROM A REFRESHING MIXTURE OF TROPICAL FRUITS,
ALL OF WHICH ARE NOW EASILY AVAILABLE IN MOST SUPERMARKETS.

Ingredients

½ cantaloupe or honeydew
melon, seeds removed

½ small pineapple

2 oranges

¼ pound fresh strawberries,
halved

1 mango, peeled and sliced

½ pound watermelon,
peeled and cubed

¼ pound guava, peeled
and cubed

½ cup superfine sugar

⅔ cup white wine

Grated rind and juice of 1 lemon

TIME Preparation takes about
45 minutes and cooking takes
about 3 minutes.

PREPARATION It is unnecessary
to remove the pips from the
watermelon unless you
particularly dislike them.

1. Using a melon baller or teaspoon,
scoop out rounds of flesh from the
cantaloupe or honeydew melon.

2. Cut the piece of pineapple in half
lengthwise and carefully peel away the
outer skin. Remove any eyes left in the
outside edge of the pineapple using a
potato peeler. Cut away the core from
the pineapple with a serrated knife and
slice the flesh thinly. Put the slices of
pineapple into a large bowl along with
the melon rounds.

3. Peel the oranges using a serrated knife.
Take care to remove all the white parts,
as they will flavor the fruit salad. Cut
the orange into segments, carefully
removing the inner membrane from the
segments as you slice.

4. Add the orange segments to the bowl
along with the strawberries, mango,
watermelon, and guava.

5. Put the sugar, wine, lemon juice, and
rind into a small saucepan and warm
through gently, stirring all the time
until the sugar has dissolved—do not
let it boil. Set aside to cool.

6. Put the syrup into the bowl along with
the fruit and mix thoroughly. Chill the
fruit salad completely before serving.

Serves 6–8

Kompot

THIS CLASSIC MIDDLE EASTERN DISH IS EASY TO PREPARE
AND CAN BE MADE WELL IN ADVANCE.

Ingredients

2 cups dried prunes

2 cups dried apricots

1 cup dried figs

1 cup raisins

1 cup blanched almonds

½ cup pine kernels

1 tsp cinnamon

¼ tsp nutmeg

½ cup brown sugar

1 tbsp rose extract (optional)

Juice and zest of 1 orange

1. Stone the prunes if necessary and chop coarsely.

2. Halve the apricots and quarter the figs.

3. Place the fruits in a large bowl and add the rest of the ingredients. Cover with cold water.

4. Stir well and keep in a cool place for 1 to 2 days, stirring a couple of times each day. Mix again before serving.

TIME Preparation takes 15 minutes. Standing time is 1 to 2 days.

SERVING IDEA Serve with yogurt or cream.

COOK'S TIP After 24 hours the liquid in which the Kompot is soaking will become very thick and syrupy. If you need to add more liquid, add a little orange juice.

VARIATION Other dried fruits may be used in the same quantities. Pistachio nuts can be substituted for the blanched almonds.

Melon *Melons are gourds, the sweetest and most succulent members of the family that embraces cucumbers, marrows, pumpkins, and watermelons. Wherever they originated (the experts are undecided between Asia and Africa), it is certain they have been eaten and enjoyed by man for over 4000 years.*

Index